LEXIS®:

A Legal Research Manual

By
Kathleen M. Carrick

Dayton, Ohio

Printed in the United States of America

Library of Congress Catalog Card Number 89-60306

ISBN 0-926578-00-6 9.95

LEXIS:

A Legal Research Manual

By
Kathleen M. Carrick

TRADEMARKS

Each of the following names is a trademark, registered trademark, or service mark of Mead Data Central, Inc. or its subsidiaries.

DEBUT™ screen/message	Mead Data Central, Inc.
Drugdex® system	Micromedex, Inc.
ECLIPSE™ feature	Mead Data Central, Inc.
Emergindex® system	Micromedex, Inc.
INCORP® library	Mead Data Central, Inc.
LEXIS® Cite	Mead Data Central, Inc.
LEXIS® Document Services	Mead Data Central, Inc.
LEXIS® service	Mead Data Central, Inc.
LEXPAT® service	Mead Data Central, Inc.
LEXSEE® feature	Mead Data Central, Inc.
LEXSTAT™ feature	Mead Data Central, Inc.
MEADNET® telecommunications network	Mead Data Central, Inc.
MEDIS® service	Mead Data Central, Inc.
NEXIS® service	Mead Data Central, Inc.
Poisindex® system	Micromedex, Inc.
UBIQ™ terminal	Mead Data Central, Inc.

Each of the following names is a trademark, registered trademark, or service mark of the company listed to the right of the name.

ABI/INFORM® Business and Management Database	Data Courier, Inc.
Alaskanet	Alascom, Inc.
American Digest System®	West Publishing Company
American Law Reports	Lawyers Cooperative Publishing Company
Auto-Cite®	VERALEX INC.
Billcast™ Legislative Forecasts	Center for the Study of Public Choice, George Mason University
Buick Skylark®	General Motors Corporation
CAN/LAW	Canada Law Book Limited
Dialog®	Dialog Information Services, Inc.
IBM	International Business Machines Corporation
IBM PC	International Business Machines Corporation
Insta-Cite®	West Publishing Company
Insurance Periodicals Index™	NILS Publishing Company
Insurlaw™	NILS Publishing Company
Legal Resource Index™	Information Access Company
Medline®	National Library of Medicine
National Insurance Law Service	NILS Publishing Company
National Reporter System®	West Publishing Company
PHINET®	Prentice Hall Information Services
QL	QL Systems Limited, Ottawa, Canada
Shepardize®	Shepard's/McGraw-Hill, Inc.
Shepard's® Citation Service	Shepard's/McGraw-Hill, Inc.
SHOWME	VERALEX INC.
Telenet	GTE Telenet Communication Corporation
Trademarkscan®	Thomson & Thomson
Tymnet	McDonnell Douglas Network Systems, Inc.
VERALEX	VERALEX, INC.
West Key Number® System	West Publishing Company
WESTLAW®	West Publishing Company

Dedicated to the memory of my mother, Genevieve.

Editor's Note

Employers want law graduates who can find the law.

Most employers use computer-assisted legal research services to complement traditional tools and expect law graduates to be able to use both.

To find the law, a lawyer must use the analytical skills gained in law school as well as the more mechanical skills of using a digest or pressing the appropriate button on a computer keyboard. The ability to use computer-assisted legal research services is evidence of the ability to reason as a lawyer. Reviewing a printout of the LEXIS search requests and the LEXIS files selected often indicates whether the researcher understood the issues and operative facts of the problem.

Mead Data Central has paid for writing and publishing this Manual because we believe legal research involves more than just pressing the appropriate button. Finding the law is an important aspect of legal reasoning.

This Manual, as the title suggests, primarily uses the LEXIS service in descriptions of computer-assisted services. Because the LEXIS service was the first of its kind and defined the central features and protocols for the services that followed, we believe the general applicability of the Manual belies its title.

fdr

About the Author

Kathleen Carrick has been the Law Librarian and Associate Professor of Law at Case Western Reserve University since 1983. Prior to that she served in the same role at the State University of New York at Buffalo. Carrick has a B.A. in Journalism from Duquesne University and worked briefly for the Plain Dealer newspaper before studying law. She has an M.L.S. from the University of Pittsburgh and a J.D. from Cleveland State University.

Table of Contents

Acknowledgements

Writing a book takes a great deal of effort and the support of many people. I appreciate the opportunity to say "thanks" to those friends and colleagues who have been vital to this Manual.

I owe a special thanks to my staff — both past and present — who worked through two years for a boss with a book on her back. In the final Manual, every member of the staff will see a reflection of a question, a statement or a thought that I raised with them during the writing process. A special debt is owed Myrna Hardy, my executive secretary, and my research assistants, Margaret Crawford and Rita Fagan. Pat Harris, my former Associate who is now the Director of the University of Missouri at Kansas City Law Library, helped as I formalized the original idea of the need for a text that would integrate traditional and computer-assisted research. Also in on the ground work of this Manual was Eve Greene, now an editor with Banks-Baldwin.

Other librarian colleagues offered their support. My Advisory Board consisted of: Harry S. Martin III, Law Librarian at Harvard University; Ralph Brill, Professor of Law and Director of Research and Writing at IIT/ Chicago-Kent College of Law; Elizabeth Evans, Reference Librarian at the New York University School of Law; and Myron Jacobstein, Law Librarian Emeritus of Stanford University. Together the Board represented a strong background in teaching legal research and helped question pedagogical approaches and practical issues. I especially appreciated Professor Jacobstein's advice to make sure the Manual included many illustrations. I am sure the students who use the Manual will also thank him for his sage counsel.

The Board was chaired by Roy Mersky, Law Librarian of the Tarlton Library of the University of Texas at Austin. In his role as educational advisor to Mead Data Central and as a continuing mentor and friend, Professor Mersky provided initial support of the Manual and valuable guidance throughout its production.

Less official, but very productive, roles were played by Gary Hartman and Christopher Simoni, also of the Tarlton Law Library. They reviewed several chapters and their comments were significant and helpful.

I would like to thank the law faculty at Case Western Reserve for their encouragement as colleagues and friends. Special thanks to Dean Peter Gerhart for his continuing support of both myself and the law library throughout the gestation of the book.

Thanks are also owed to law librarian friends who were always available for help, comments or a shoulder to cry on. They include: Joyce Saltalamachia, Law Librarian at the New York Law School; Robert Nissenbaum, Law Librarian at Loyola University School of Law, Los Angeles; Donald Dunn, Law Librarian at Western New England College of Law; Carol Roehrenbeck, Law Librarian at Nova

University; and Lolly Gasaway, Law Librarian at the University of North Carolina.

Basic to the effort were the folks from Mead Data Central. I owe thanks to George Relles and Chris Coyle — the guys in charge who believed in the idea of a Manual on integrated legal research and supported it with their budgets. Many thanks to Marsha Diamond, Mead's National Law School Director, for her input on law school curricula. The creative skills of Lisa Bear, Rob Markey, and Linda Sowers were essential to the quality of the Manual. Leigh Sempeles was one of the original editors who helped in the formative drafting and Ed Poster served as the clean-up man, pulling the final manuscript together. I was consistently impressed with the staff at MDC and their dedication to the production of a quality educational Manual.

My greatest appreciation is due to my main Mead Data Central editor, Buzz Reed. Involved in the Manual from its inception, his intelligence, thorough knowledge of the LEXIS and NEXIS services, wit and humanity assured the Manual quality and taught me a great deal. He did not make it easy, but he made it good. Thanks, Buzz.

Finally, thanks to my family, who believed in it.

Kathleen M. Carrick

Preface

Most law schools introduced computer-assisted legal research (CALR) into their curriculum during the 1970's. The novelty and mysticism of computers were replaced quickly by an appreciation that a revolution was taking place in legal research.

Today, almost every law school in the United States trains its students in the use of computer-assisted legal research. However, most schools continue to isolate computer-assisted research from traditional research, artificially presenting computers as decorative icing on the cake of traditional bibliographic sources. Such legal research programs fail to integrate computer-assisted legal research properly and lack an accurate image of how more and more of today's attorneys are performing research.

These failures in the curriculum are due, somewhat, to existing legal research and writing textbooks, which isolate computer-assisted legal research ("CALR") tools. Although CALR is vaguely alluded to, it is usually only described in a separate chapter talking about the "how to" instead of the "why." This gap in the treatment of CALR leaves the student viewing traditional tools and CALR as competing forces that one must choose between.

The major purpose of this Manual is to begin to fill this gap by demonstrating how CALR relates to the total research process. Since it is a first attempt to integrate legal databases and traditional resources, this Manual is arranged in a format that is similar to traditional legal research textbooks. It can be used as an addition to traditional texts and is not intended to be comprehensive in its coverage. Other excellent texts perform that function. Rather it focuses on the main areas where legal databases should be learned in conjunction with their traditional hardcopy counterparts.

This Manual is also meant to help instructors as they face the challenge of integrating legal databases with traditional sources. The hypothetical problems, sample questions and related readings aid the adaption of the Manual into traditional research curricula.

This Manual's ultimate goal is to help the student become more analytical in performing legal research. When faced with a legal issue, the ultimate test of your legal skill of researching will be the selection of the best sources and approaches to reach a solution quickly and accurately. When you can understand the relationships between computer-assisted legal research and traditional resources, you will be able to use both sources to their maximum potential. And after all, isn't potential what law school is all about?

Introduction

A Lawyer's Duty to Research

Welcome to legal research. As a graduate student in a professional school you might wonder why your first-year program contains a course dedicated to research. You did not need to take a special course on the research process as an undergraduate. Why not just pick up the research skills as you go?

The answer is that as an attorney you will be responsible for knowing the law — a process of identifying and understanding the possible legal implications of your client's position. You cannot do this without legal research.

Most law school courses deal with substantive areas of law like Torts and Contracts. These classes help you begin to "think like a lawyer" and teach you the concepts and issues dealt with by lawyers. However, these courses can only begin to help you build the base of knowledge of substantive law that an attorney needs to practice law competently.

Even if you could learn all the law related to a particular type of practice, the substantive law constantly changes. Merely referring to class notes or to a casebook is not an acceptable method of legal research. The day after you finish your Torts course a new statute or court decision may alter a doctrine that has existed for decades. Imagine the apprehension felt by a recent graduate of a law school's Masters in Taxation program after the passage of the monumental tax code revision in 1986. After 15 courses in taxation and the reading of hundreds of tax cases, the graduate faced the challenge of dealing with a sweeping revision of tax law.

Your Professional Responsibility

The most important reason to learn how to perform legal research is that soon someone will rely on your knowledge of the law and your legal advice. The Model Rules of Professional Conduct of the American Bar Association clearly state the attorney's duty to represent a client competently.[1] Courts also have recognized this professional obligation. The Supreme Court of California, in *Smith v. Lewis,*[2] allowed a judgment against an attorney who was found to be negligent in his research.

The California court wrote: ". . . we believe an attorney assumes an obligation to his client to undertake reasonable research in an effort to ascertain relevant legal principles and to make an informed decision as to a course of conduct. . ."[3].

This book explores the complementary uses of traditional tools and online services in modern legal research.

Unless you have worked in the legal field, your first tour of the school's law library will expose you to unfamiliar books and databases that you never knew existed. Legal research involves the use of sources such as statutes, judicial decisions and administrative regulations found in books as well as online databases like the LEXIS service. Learning to use the traditional sources and online databases is a basic skill that every attorney must learn.

As a recent article in *The National Law Journal* stated, "Lawyers who do not know what LEXIS and WESTLAW offer are practicing law with blinders. They will suffer what they deserve."[4]

You must base the advice you provide and the legal actions you take on behalf of your client on a clear and precise understanding of all the legal principles involved in the case. Thorough and accurate research using the most efficient tools will help you advise your client. Your continuing professional responsibility includes a duty to be aware of developments in legal research and to use the most appropriate research tools available to you. This book explores the complementary uses of traditional tools and online services in modern legal research.

Legal Research — the Search for Primary and Secondary Authorities

Legal research is the process of identifying and weighing sources or "authorities." You cannot separate the two tasks of finding authorities and determining their relevance. You will use principles and doctrines of the United States legal system to ascertain the

---

[1]Rule 1.1 states: "A lawyer shall provide competent representation to a client. Competent representation requires the legal knowledge, skill, thoroughness and preparation reasonably necessary for the representation."

[2]Smith v. Lewis, 13 Cal.3d 349, 118 Cal. Rptr. 621, 530 P.2d 589 (1975), *overruled on other grounds,* In re Marriage of Brown, 15 Cal.3d 838, 126 Cal.Rptr. 633, 544 P.2d 561 (1976).

[3]*Id.* at 359. *Smith* is further explored in Richards, *Lawyer Malpractice — The Duty to Perform Legal Research,* 32 Fed'n Ins. Counsel Q. 199-207 (1982). *See also,* Aloy v. Mash, 38 Cal. 3d 413, 212 Cal. Rptr. 162, 696 P.2d 656 (1985).

[4]Harrington, *Use of LEXIS and WESTLAW Too Is Vital to Any Law Practice,* Nat'l L. J. Oct. 12, 1987, at 18, col. 3.

relevance and merit of the authorities you discover in the course of your research.

Primary authorities are statements documenting the legal actions of courts, legislatures and administrative agencies. *Secondary* authorities discuss or interpret the law found in primary authorities. Additional basic principles of our legal system will guide your use of primary and secondary authorities.

Primary Authority

Constitutions, statutes, court decisions, and administrative rules and regulations are examples of primary authorities.

Regard a statute, rule or decision produced by the highest court or legislative body within a jurisdiction as "mandatory" primary authority which must be followed. For example, in most matters of state law, the pertinent statute passed by the state legislature, rules or regulations of various state agencies, and any decisions of higher state courts will bind a court. It is imperative that you identify any mandatory primary authority that applies to your legal research.

Consider primary authority from another jurisdiction as persuasive, but not mandatory. If you can argue that the courts or legislature within your jurisdiction have not dealt with your issues, you may not have mandatory primary authority to follow. At other times you may argue that your jurisdiction's primary authority is weak or erroneous and should be changed. In both situations you might refer to primary authority from other jurisdictions to support your argument.

On a question of Illinois law . . .

PRIMARY AUTHORITIES

Mandatory

- **Illinois Statutes**
- **Decisions of the Illinois Supreme Court**
- **U.S. Constitution**
- **Illinois Constitution**

Persuasive

- **Cases from other states**
- **Cases from lower Illinois courts**

Case Law as Primary Authority

Several basic legal principles govern the importance of a case to your legal research problem. You may have heard a case referred to as a "precedent." The dictionary defines precedent as "a thing or person that goes before another."[5] When people know the predictable consequences of an action like getting married, entering into a contract, or robbing a bank, they can make informed decisions. It would be unfair for a court to handle one situation differently from another with similar circumstances. The common law doctrine of stare decisis requires courts within the same jurisdiction to follow prior court decisions dealing with the same point of law.

Stare decisis (Latin for "to stand by decided matters")[6] evolved in medieval England as the kings centralized their power by creating a court system that would assure similar treatment of like cases. It remains a basic principle of law and the primary reason why you must identify all applicable court decisions in your research.

Decisions are based on prior decisions

[5] THE OXFORD ENGLISH DICTIONARY 1243 (1933).

[6] WEBSTER'S NEW INTERNATIONAL DICTIONARY 2459 (2d ed. 1936).

Courts have been writing decisions for centuries, creating opinions that are sometimes still relevant and authoritative. Some court decisions, like *Marbury v. Madison*,[7] are landmark cases. *Marbury's* holding that the U.S. Supreme Court had the power to review Acts of Congress and declare them void if contrary to the Constitution continues to control legal decisions.

When your research has identified a case, you must read it carefully to differentiate between dicta and the real holding or law of the case. Dicta are statements included in a court opinion which are not necessary to the basic holding of the decision. Dicta can consist of hypothetical discussions of issues that have not appeared in the case. Dicta also can be opinions of a judge which do not address the central decision. Dicta do not bind a court under the doctrine of stare decisis.

Statutes as Primary Authority

Statutes are another source of primary authority, which the legislative branch of government enacts. Statutes are mandatory authority — they must be followed — in their own jurisdiction.

Just as with case law, various principles govern the interpretation of statutes. For example, you may look at the intent of the legislators as you apply statutes to particular situations.

Legislation tries to anticipate legal problems and establish rules prospectively for dealing with problems. In comparison, court decisions confront distinct fact situations and settle particular disputes which have occurred.

Legislative language is often general, providing the courts with the important role of interpreting statutes and applying them to specific facts or issues. You cannot view a statute in a vacuum. Your legal research must consider court decisions which analyze or consider the validity of a pertinent statute. Statutory research involves identifying the applicable statutes as well as the court decisions which interpret or apply the statutes.

Executive and Administrative Sources of Primary Authority

The U.S. Constitution[8] vests the executive power of the government in the President. As chief executive of the United States, the President may issue Executive Orders which are primary authority. At the state level, similar authority is vested in the governor.

Administrative agencies are relatively new producers of primary authority. The "New Deal" in the 1930's and the "Great Society" of the 1960's spawned most of the agencies that now comprise the federal executive branch of government. Most of the federal

---

[7]Marbury v. Madison, 5 U.S. (1 Cranch) 137 (1803).

[8]U.S. CONST. Art. II, §1, cl. 1.

agencies oversee specialized areas of governmental activity. Congress creates an agency by passing an "enabling statute" that broadly outlines the agency's powers and responsibilities.[9]

The agencies promulgate rules and regulations to detail the statutes the agencies enforce. For example, the Secretary of Interior has issued regulations determining the applicability of state and local regulations on the use of Indian property. These regulations are based on the laws that enable agencies to establish regulations and that give the Commissioner of Indian Affairs the duty to manage all Indian affairs.[10]

Agencies promulgate rules and regulations to add detail to the statutes.

The agency not only makes the regulations but enforces and interprets them, a unique combination of legislative and judicial roles. If there is any dispute over these regulations or if a party is accused of disobeying the regulations, the agency's administrative judges will issue a ruling to interpret and enforce the rules.

There is some debate whether agency decisions are mandatory authority or merely persuasive. Purists argue that the agencies are not bound by stare decisis. Practitioners who work with the agencies recognize that the precedential value of prior administrative decisions can vary, with some agencies guided more by political exigency than stare decisis.

Summary of Primary Authority

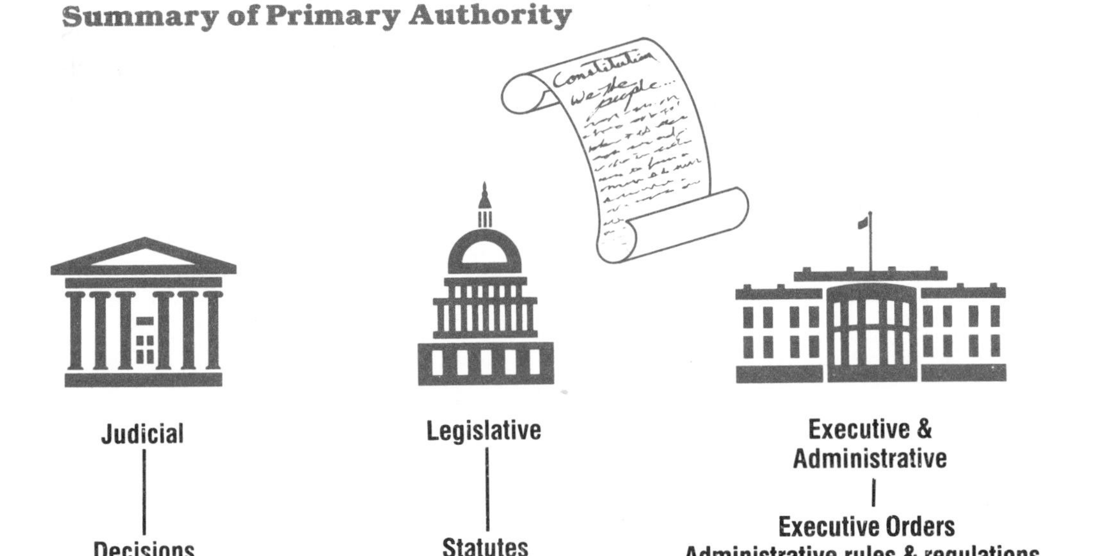

[9] K.C. Davis, The Administrative Process 2 (1977).

[10] The enabling statutes can be found at 5 U.S.C. § 301 (1982) and 25 U.S.C. § 2 (1982). The regulations are at 25 C.F.R. § 1.4 (1987). 5 U.S.C. § 301 (1982) reads: "The head of an Executive department or military department may prescribe regulations for the government of his department, the conduct of its employees, the distribution and performance of its business, and the custody, use, and preservation of its records, papers, and property."

Secondary Authority

Sources which comment upon or discuss the law are secondary authorities. Secondary authorities can be extremely helpful by providing background information and offering a viewpoint when it can be argued that there is no primary authority that must be followed.

To distinguish between primary and secondary authorities, analyze the source.

You will use secondary authorities such as law reviews, encyclopedias and legal dictionaries as you use their non-legal counterparts: to point you to other works, to furnish a general introduction to an unknown subject, or to define a word. Secondary authorities such as hornbooks, treatises and law reviews discuss areas of law and are particularly helpful when you could reasonably draw different conclusions from the primary authorities. These sources provide information that might persuade a court to consider a scholar's commentary or to recognize a developing doctrine that could support your client's position.

Law review case notes or *American Law Reports* annotations provide the most detailed, and often the most timely, editorial analysis of court decisions. Usually the opinions of recognized scholars as expressed in treatises or articles are the only secondary authority courts consider in their deliberations.

To distinguish between primary and secondary authorities, analyze the source of the authority. To identify primary authority, ask yourself if an individual, court, legislative body or administrative agency is making the law in that jurisdiction. To identify secondary authority, ask yourself if a scholar or editor is commenting on, interpreting or summarizing the law.

Reference or Finding Tools

Much of legal research involves reading. Often you find authorities by reading authorities. For example, a case may cite to other cases, statutes and regulations. But legal research also involves other legal reference and finding tools which help you find primary and secondary authorities. These include tools which are similar to the indexes and digests you might have used in other disciplines as well as more specialized guides designed specifically for legal research.

Legal databases include both primary and secondary authorities.

Legal databases such as the LEXIS service serve dual roles as finding tools and as repositories of primary and secondary authorities. Sometimes you will use a legal database to find authorities and other times you will use a legal database to read authorities you already have identified.

Legal Research: Evolution & Revolution

The Evolution in Legal Publication

As the common law developed, a lawyer's knowledge of precedent depended upon word of mouth or memory. There was little or no record of cases and no method existed for finding the text of a court decision. The development of printing technology allowed case reports to be compiled and widely distributed.

The early colonists brought English law, its doctrines, and law reports to America. Although law books were scarce during the colonial period, the growth of the new government assured the evolution of legal publishing in America. [11] The English system of writing and distributing court opinions flourished as federal and state court systems grew. Statutes, administrative rules and regulations added to the proliferation of legal information as the United States became an industrial giant and a world power.[12]

The evolving federal, state and municipal governments recognized their responsibilities to make the law available to the public in written form, but often were not equipped to provide editorial enhancements to the raw information. Private publishers saw the need for order and introduced systems which attempted to organize and index legal materials to make them accessible to the profession on a timely basis.

The Revolution: Computer-Assisted Legal Research

By the late 1960's the growth of legal information made it difficult to find the law.[13]

The U.S. Supreme Court disposes of more than 4,000 cases each year.

Traditional indexing systems, often outdated or too general, failed to keep pace with new vocabulary and technology. Sometimes indexes included new legal concepts under old generic top-

---

[11]J. Parrish, *Law Books and Legal Publishing in America 1760 - 1840*, 72 L. Lib. J. 355 (1979).

[12]There are many books dealing with the history of American law. Among the most popular: L. Friedman, A History of American Law (1973) and G. Gilmore, The Ages of American Law (1977).

[13]Several statistics reported in the *Annual Report of The Director of The Administrative Office of The United States Courts* (1987) may assist you in understanding the quantity of federal case law produced each year (these figures do not include cases before state courts). About 20,000 trials are completed in the federal district courts each year. *Id.* at 123. More than 25,000 cases are pending before the U.S. Courts of Appeals and each year more than 8,000 cases are concluded on the merits after submission of briefs. *Id.* at 138. The U.S. Supreme Court disposes of more than 4,000 cases each year. The Supreme Court disposes of about 170 cases by full opinions each term. Several hundred cases remain on the docket of the U.S. Supreme Court at the end of each term. *Id.* at 135. As you will learn later in this book, case law represents only a portion of the law created each year.

ics.[14] How could traditional systems report and index the proliferation of new cases, statutes and regulations?[15]

Concerned attorneys recognized these problems and began to explore avenues of new technology that were already rapidly changing the handling of non-legal information. The Ohio State Bar Association began investigating the feasibility of computer-assisted legal research. In 1967, the Ohio Bar organized a non-profit organization, called the Ohio Bar Automated Research (OBAR) to develop a practical, online legal database.

OBAR decided that a successful legal database system would contain the full text of the law and be interactive with the individual legal researcher. Such a system would allow you, the lawyer, to be in control of the research process. You would identify and select words and issues, phrasing them in the language of the law. This process of connecting words to construct a search strategy followed Boolean logic, a system named after a 19th century mathematician. By searching the full text of cases for chosen words and phrases, your dependency on indexes would be minimized.

The OBAR standard of full-text search and retrieval offered a powerful tool. The researcher could customize his or her research by finding any mention of a fact, a phrase or an issue that might appear in an opinion or other legal document. For example, cases on the enforcement of school dress codes may involve several very different aspects of substantive law. In the late 1960's an attorney using traditional research tools could find all such cases only by thinking of all the substantive legal topics. How often an attorney must have wished just to find all cases that contained the phrase "dress code!"

"...filed this suit seeking injun
t that the dress code in regard
nited States Constitution. ..."

Before computer-assisted research, an attorney could not search for cases containing the phrase "dress code."

The LEXIS service, based on the lessons of the OBAR system, was introduced in 1973. Since that time, the LEXIS service has led the way in full-text data retrieval and has revolutionized legal research. It is now used by members of the bar in several countries, including the United States, England and France. Large and small law firms as well as federal and state courts use the LEXIS service daily to find the law.

In the late 1970's West Publishing Company also introduced an online database of legal materials known as "WESTLAW." Originally the WESTLAW database contained only West editors' summaries of cases, but later expanded to include full text.

Today, the use of online services is incorporated with the basic research skills you learn throughout law school.

---

[14] *See supra p. 51.*

[15] For a more detailed discussion of the pros and cons of the traditional legal digest systems, *see* M. Cohen & R. Berring, How to Find the Law, 122-128 (8th ed., 1983); R. Berring, *Full-Text Databases and Legal Research: Backing Into the Future*, 1 High Tech. L.J. 27 at 33-37 (1986).

Summary

This Manual explores the use of traditional tools and online services in modern legal research. As an attorney you will need to identify the best sources for your research. In the past, legal research has been taught in segments, beginning with a thorough introduction to the traditional resources. As a secondary exercise the student received training in computer-assisted legal research. This text integrates the two approaches so that you learn how the traditional resources and computer-assisted legal research complement each other.[16] Several good textbooks primarily address the use of traditional legal research tools. This text often will refer you to existing texts for additional information on the use of the traditional tools.

Traditional and computer-assisted legal research complement each other.

This chapter introduces you to the importance of legal research and the use of basic legal concepts in finding the law. It provides you with background in the traditional publication of legal materials and the development of full-text online searching capabilities. The next chapter discusses the structures of the American legal system and the LEXIS service, basic concepts important to understanding and conducting legal research.

RELATED READINGS

M. JACOBSTEIN & R. MERSKY, FUNDAMENTALS OF LEGAL RESEARCH 1 - 8 (1987 ed.).
M. COHEN & R. BERRING, HOW TO FIND THE LAW 1 - 15 (8th ed. 1983).
C. KUNZ et al., THE PROCESS OF LEGAL RESEARCH 1 - 4 (1986).

---

[16] An interesting commentary is R. Berring, *Legal Research and Legal Concepts: Where Form Molds Substance*, 75 CALIF. L. REV. 15-27 (1987).

Sources of the Law

Lawyers performing legal research take a somewhat different approach from undergraduates performing library research. Instead of starting with the card catalog, lawyers often go directly to the type of material they want, such as statutes, cases or administrative rulings.

Whether you begin your legal research by going to shelves of books or by signing on to a computer, you first should know the types of legal materials you want to find. This chapter will assist you in understanding the sources of the law by providing background on the institutions and processes that produce primary authority.

Court Structure and Process

American court systems have a tiered appellate structure in which higher courts review the actions of lower courts. Most legal research is performed by reading the reports of the opinions of the appellate courts. Appellate court opinions constitute a very small portion of the paper record generated by a lawsuit.

Court action begins with the trial court, sometimes called the court of first instance. This is the court popularized in television legal battles, where the attorneys may plead their case to a jury. As you may already know, most of the evidence has been produced and seen by both parties well before the trial. The pretrial process can create a substantial volume of legal documentation which is of limited use to anyone other than the parties to the suit.

The losing party at the trial level usually has the right to appeal the decision to a higher court within the same jurisdiction. Only certain elements of the trial court's action are reviewable on appeal. The appellate court reviews the record of the lower court for a mistake that would require it to overturn the lower court decision. The record of the trial court usually consists of the opinion, motions, pleadings, arguments of counsel and a transcript of the proceedings.

Many unpublished decisions are reported in legal databases.

Not all court opinions are published in printed reporters. For many jurisdictions no trial court opinions are published. In comparison, appellate court decisions usually are published. Many unpublished decisions, however, are available in legal databases.[1]

The value of unpublished cases as precedent varies from court to court. Often you must consult the rules of the court to determine if an unpublished opinion may be cited as precedent in that court.[2]

Federal Courts

The trial courts for most cases in the federal court system are the federal district courts. The individual district courts are named for the geographic area that they cover, such as the United States District Court for the Southern District of New York. All states have at least one district court and large states have several.

There are four federal district courts in New York.

Congress also has created specialized federal courts to handle disputes in particular areas of law. Litigation in these areas of law is often highly technical and best handled by specialized courts and judges. The bankruptcy courts and U.S. Court of International Trade are examples of such specialty courts. Some federal administrative agencies can act as trial-level courts in the federal system for matters within the regulatory authority of the agency.

The intermediate federal courts of appeal are the U.S. circuit courts. Eleven of the circuit courts hear appeals from the federal district courts. For example, a decision from the U.S. District Court for the Southern District of New York could be appealed to the U.S. Court of Appeals for the Second Circuit which has jurisdiction over all of the federal district courts in the states of New York, Connecticut and Vermont. The Court of Appeals for the District of Columbia hears appeals from the D.C. District Court and, in addition, from federal administrative agencies. The recently-created Court of Appeals for the Federal Circuit hears appeals from specialized subject courts.

The Court of Appeals for the Second Circuit hears appeals from district courts in Connecticut, New York and Vermont.

Each federal district court is within a circuit and must follow the precedent of that circuit. Because the intermediate appellate courts can differ on a point of law, federal circuit court decisions from an-

---

[1]Courts and the legal profession may use the words *unpublished* and *unreported* with different meanings. In this book the phrase *unpublished* opinion means an opinion that is not printed and distributed in a book, and the phrase *unreported* opinion means one that is neither included in a book nor a publicly-available database. Many *unpublished* decisions are *reported* in the legal databases.

[2]For more information on the use of unpublished decisions, run a LEXIS search through the text of law reviews, e.g.,

TRANSMIT: *unpublished* OR *unreported* W/15 *precedent!*

See also R. POSNER, THE FEDERAL COURTS 120-24 (1985); Reynolds & Richmond, *An Evaluation of Limited Publication in the United States Courts of Appeals: The Price of Reform*, 48 U. CHI. L. REV. 573 (1981); Weaver, George M., *The Precedential Value of Unpublished Judicial Opinions*, 39 MERCER L. REV. 477 (1988); *U.S. Appeals Court Restricts Use of Opinions by Lawyers*, N.Y. TIMES, Feb. 21, 1983, at B1.

other circuit may be cited as persuasive, but not necessarily as mandatory, authority within your circuit.

The United States Supreme Court is the final level of appeal in the federal and state court systems. Since the U.S. Supreme Court is the highest court, its holdings are mandatory primary authority for all courts. Therefore Supreme Court opinions, and even briefs and arguments, are essential resources for research.[3]

2

State Courts

The trial and appellate court systems of the states are similar to the federal court system. However, the names of courts can be very confusing. Ohio and Pennsylvania call their trial courts Courts of Common Pleas, while some of the New York trial courts are known as Supreme Courts. Make sure you check the name and the level of the court for state cases you find in your research.[4]

The opinions of state trial courts rarely are published or included in online databases.[5]

Slightly more than half of the states have intermediate courts of appeal.[6] These generally are the larger states in which the volume of litigation requires an intermediate appellate process to relieve the heavy load of appeals borne by the highest court of the state. The highest state court usually is called the "supreme court" and its holdings are mandatory authority for the lower courts of that state. Most state appellate decisions are published or reported in online databases.[7] However, because of the expense of buying and maintaining the reporter sets individually or as part of the National Reporter System, many libraries do not have published reports of cases from all 50 states.

---

[3]For more information on the structure of the federal courts, *see* B. LAWRENCE, AMERICAN COURTS: PROCESS AND POLICY (1986). Several articles discuss the caseload and the expansion of the federal appellate court system, e.g., Baker & McFarland, *The Need for a New National Court*, 100 HARV. L. REV. 1400 (1987); Ginsburg and Huber, *The Intercircuit Panel*, 100 HARV. L. REV. 1417 (1987).

[4]For a table of state courts and case reporters, *see* A UNIFORM SYSTEM OF CITATION, at section H, 177-217 (14th ed. 1986).

[5]For example, the opinion of the state trial court in the Baby "M" case is one of a few trial court decisions from New Jersey that have been published in a printed reporter or included in an online service. *Re Baby "M"*, 217 N.J. Super. 313, 525 A2d 1128 (1987) *aff'd in part and rev'd in part by* 109 N.J. 396, 1988 N.J. LEXIS 1, 537 A.2d 1227 (1988). Trial court decisions for some states, such as New York, are more likely to be included in published reporters and the LEXIS service.

[6]THE BOOK OF STATES (1988-89 ed. 1988). As of 1988, there were 37 states with intermediate appellate courts: Alabama, Alaska, Arizona, Arkansas, California, Colorado, Connecticut, Florida, Georgia, Hawaii, Idaho, Illinois, Indiana, Iowa, Kansas, Kentucky, Louisiana, Maryland, Massachusetts, Michigan, Minnesota, Missouri, New Jersey, New Mexico, New York, North Carolina, Ohio, Oklahoma, Oregon, Pennsylvania, South Carolina, Tennessee, Texas, Utah, Virginia, Washington and Wisconsin.

[7]In addition, the LEXIS service includes unpublished appellate opinions from several states.

The Relationship Between Federal and State Courts

There are many instances in which federal courts apply state law.

The relationship between the state and federal courts is intrinsic to the system of federalism and a central topic in several of your law school courses. You will gain a better understanding of the separate jurisdictions of state and federal courts in your other courses. There are many instances in which federal courts apply state law, and therefore you may search federal cases for references to issues of state law. There also are many instances in which state courts interpret the federal constitution and statutes, so you may search state cases for references to the Constitution and federal statutes. Thus you may search more than one LEXIS library or use more than one traditional tool to cover all the courts that may interpret your issue.

Legislative Structure and Process

The interpretation of statutes often involves not only scrutiny of the wording of the statute but also an inquiry into the intent of the legislature when it enacted the statute. Therefore a brief review of the legislative process may be helpful. The path of a bill introduced in the U.S. Senate is described below to illustrate the process.

The Federal Legislature

The interpretation of a statute often involves an inquiry into the intent of the legislature.

The United States Congress consists of two houses, the Senate and the House of Representatives. Any member of either house can introduce a bill.[8] You can trace a bill as it passes through the legislature by using the bill number which is assigned when the bill is introduced. For example, "S.1" indicates the first Senate bill introduced during a session.

After introduction, the bill is assigned to the standing committee with jurisdiction over the subject of the bill. Usually a subcommittee studies the bill. If there is sufficient interest, the subcommittee holds hearings and reports to the full committee. The committee votes on whether to table the bill or send it to the Senate for consideration. If the bill is sent to the Senate for debate, the committee submits a report describing the bill and including the committee's recommendations.

Then the full Senate debates and votes on the bill. If the bill passes the Senate, the House of Representatives receives the final version and the bill proceeds through another series of committee considerations, including hearings, debates and voting. If the House passes a bill that varies from the Senate bill, a conference committee composed of members from both houses attempts to develop a compromise.

---

[8] Appropriation bills can originate only in the House of Representatives.

Once the same bill passes both houses, it is sent to the President, who can elect to sign the bill into law, veto it, or allow it to become law without presidential signature.[9]

Often statutes simply modify or revoke prior acts of the legislature. A typical new law may merely change the phrase "16 percent" to "18 percent" in an existing law. After the new law is passed, it must be integrated into the prior laws. A collection of current laws is called a *code*. A code compiles the existing laws for a jurisdiction by subject.

The bills, hearings, reports in all versions, floor debates and the statutes themselves constitute the legislative history of statutes and may be used to apply or interpret the law. Many law libraries have these congressional documents in hard copy or microfiche. The LEXIS service also includes a selection of legislative history.

An example of legislative documentation is the *Congressional Record*, the daily publication of congressional proceedings. You can use the *Congressional Record*'s transcripts of floor debates to determine what the legislators intended a statute to accomplish. Your library probably has the *Congressional Record* in hard copy and it also is available on both of the major online services. The NEXIS service, which includes the full text of *The New York Times, Washington Post*, and *Daily Report for Executives*, is another good source for legislative history as well as for information about current legislative action.[10]

State Legislatures

State legislatures follow processes similar to Congress to enact statutes. The laws of each state also are codified and published. The LEXIS service now includes the codes of approximately half the states. There is little published documentation of most state legislative activity prior to passage of a bill, making research into legislative intent comparatively difficult. You probably will rely more on press acounts in newspapers and wire stories to find the legislative histories of state statutes.

The Executive Branch

The President, as executive leader of the United States government, has the authority to sign treaties and issue regulations and executive orders. But, for the most part, the President creates law indirectly. The President influences the legislative process by issu-

---

[9]For a more complete discussion of the process by which a bill becomes law, *see* E. WILLETT, HOW OUR LAWS ARE MADE (1986).

[10]The NEXIS service is described in Chapter Seven. Your school's special educational subscription for the LEXIS service may not include these files.

ing statements, making speeches and sending messages to Congress. The President also nominates Supreme Court Justices and federal judges.

Administrative Structure and Process

Although there are three branches of government — executive, judicial and legislative — the "unofficial" fourth branch consisting of administrative agencies under the executive is one of the most powerful and pervasive in making law. Many attorneys devote a substantial portion of their practice to administrative law. Knowledge of the structure and processes of administrative agencies will assist you in understanding the sources of administrative law.

Federal Administrative Law and Procedure

The administrative branch undertakes to implement the policies the legislative branch has described in the enabling statute. In 1887 Congress created the first major federal regulatory agency, the Interstate Commerce Commission, to take on the more detailed tasks of regulating rates of railroads.[11] In this century federal and state statutes have created numerous administrative agencies.

Administrative agencies fulfill their regulatory missions by various means. Agencies publish proposed rules and regulations, allowing comments by public and private parties before determining the final regulation. Comments received from public and private parties assist in determining the final regulations. But administrative agencies make law by means other than issuing regulations. Like legislators, administrative authorities cannot anticipate the full range of circumstances that regulations eventually will cover. Many administrative agencies have the power to enforce and adjudicate alleged violations of the regulations they have promulgated. Nearly 1,100 federal administrative law judges (ALJ's) handle more than 400,000 hearings each year for 30 agencies.[12] Federal statutes set forth the practices and procedures of federal administrative proceedings.[13]

The different roles agencies play in making law results in regulations, licenses, rulings and administrative decisions.

The different roles agencies play in making law result in different sources of administrative law — regulations, licenses, rulings and administrative decisions. The federal government publishes some, but not all, of the law produced by agencies. The LEXIS

---

[11]Interstate Commerce Commission Act, 24 Stat. 379, 49 U.S.C. §§ 501 - 507 (1887).

[12]*Breaking Away: ALJ's Seek Freer Status*, 71 A.B.A. J. 18 (1985).

[13]Administrative Procedure Act, ch. 324, 60 Stat. 237 (1946) *(as codified and amended by 5 U.S.C.* §§ 551 - 559, 701 - 706, 3105 - 3344 (1982)).

service includes most of the published sources as well as unpublished sources. Chapter Six provides you more detail on where to find federal administrative law.

State Administrative Law and Procedure

State agencies have responsibilities, structures and processes that are very similar to their federal counterparts. Many states publish regulations and administrative decisions, but often the published versions are difficult to identify and obtain. That difficulty has been eased to some extent as some state administrative materials have been added to the LEXIS service.

Unravelling the Law

Courts, legislatures, executive officers and administrative agencies are all sources of primary authority. Your responsibility as an attorney will be to identify pertinent decisions, statutes, rules and regulations, and to apply them to legal issues. But to interpret the law you will have to do more than find a statute or a case or a regulation. The issues and particular circumstances of a legal problem can invoke different sources of law. To interpret the law you will actually "unravel" the law as it has been created by the interactions among the various branches of government. The interactions among the branches to produce the law do not follow a particular order.

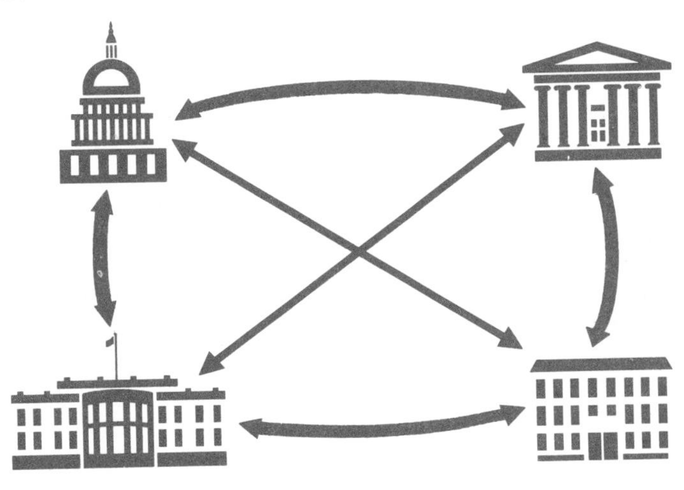

The interactions among the branches to produce the law do not follow a particular order.

For example, Congress may pass a statute and an agency may promulgate regulations that clarify the application of the statute. If a lawsuit arises, a court may interpret both the enabling statute and the regulations. One of the parties may raise a constitutional issue. If a portion of the statute or regulation is declared unconstitutional by the court, Congress may react by amending the statute to satisfy the constitutional requirements. If you research only the statutes, you will not be able to describe to your client the entire picture of how the statute may be applied.

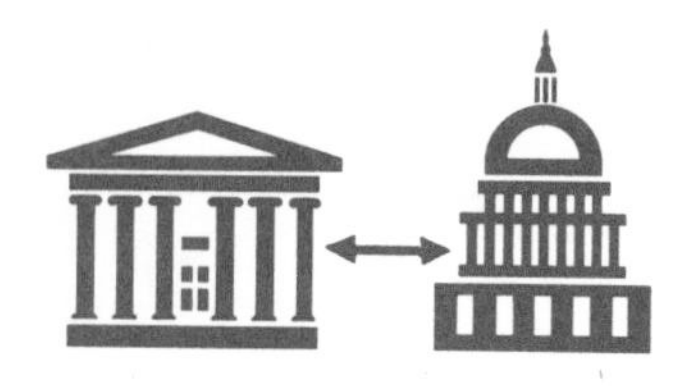

As another example, for many years courts have held that the losing party is not responsible for the legal fees of the winning party. Recently, however, legislatures have enacted statutes changing the ground rules of litigation and shifting the burden of the attorneys' fees in some situations. If your research finds only the common law as stated in cases, your research may be incomplete.

Unravelling the interactions of the branches of government and assessing the probability of future actions is one of the most intellectually challenging aspects of legal research.

The Structure of LEXIS Libraries and Files

Law libraries and online services generally organize the law by source — case law here, statutes over there, and so on. For example, opinions of the Massachusetts Supreme Judicial Court are printed in a series titled *Massachusetts Reports* and also are arranged together in the LEXIS service. The *Delaware Revised Code* is printed in a set of volumes and arranged together in the LEXIS service.

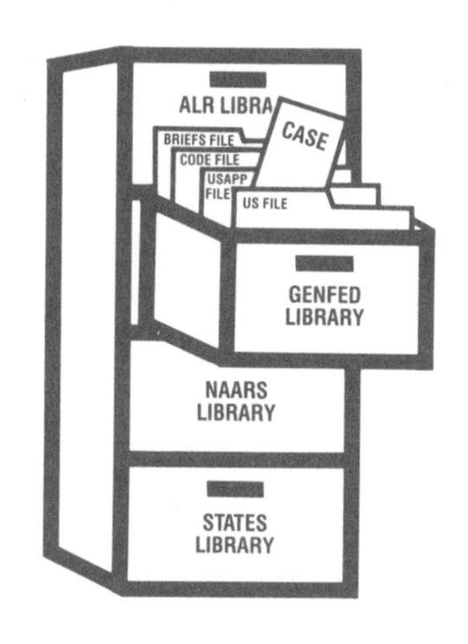

You begin research on the LEXIS service by choosing the library and then the file or files that you will search.

The LEXIS service organizes materials into broad categories called *libraries*. To begin legal research in a law library you go to the appropriate shelves. To begin your LEXIS search you first choose a library. For example, select the General Federal (GENFED) library to gain access to a broad grouping of files containing federal primary and secondary authorities.

LEXIS libraries are made up of *files* — a narrower collection of information based on source or jurisdiction. After you choose a library, select a file to search. For example, if you select the GENFED library and then the DIST file, you have narrowed your search to federal district court opinions.

Computers provide unique flexibility when it comes to choosing where to perform your legal research. For example, you may search just for federal district court decisions by choosing the DIST file. Or, you may search for federal district court decisions in combination with other federal courts by choosing a group file called COURTS. The coverage of a traditional research tool cannot be organized and reorganized at the whim of the researcher. However, computers allow you the flexibility to expand or contract the coverage of your research. Of course, because you have more choices, you also need a good understanding of the type of materials you want to find. This chapter, combined with your other course work, should help you identify the right sources for your research.[14]

2

Summary

When you begin research you need to identify the type of information you expect to find. You need a basic understanding of the structure and operation of the branches of government in order to know where to look for appropriate authorities. It also is important for you to understand how the interactions of the three branches of government flow together to form the law, in order to provide a complete picture of the legal implications of your client's problem.

RELATED READINGS

M. JACOBSTEIN & R. MERSKY, FUNDAMENTALS OF LEGAL RESEARCH 12 - 28, 141 - 147 (1987 ed.).
M. COHEN & R. BERRING, HOW TO FIND THE LAW 17 - 26 (8th ed. 1983).

[14]The *LEXIS/NEXIS* *LIBRARY CONTENTS AND ALPHABETICAL LIST OF FILES* is useful in helping you decide where to conduct your LEXIS research. Ask your librarian for a copy.

Three Hypothetical Situations

Concepts of legal research mean much more if applied to specific examples. The three scenarios described on this page will be used throughout this Manual to explain characteristics of legal research materials and the LEXIS service.

The Billboard Problem

Your client, an advertising executive in California, wants legal advice. His agency wants to place billboards along the interstate highway that runs next to an Indian reservation. Although the Indian tribe is eager to lease their land to your client, environmental interest groups and the state of California oppose the project. The interest groups claim that the billboards will deface the raw beauty of the countryside. The state of California has refused your client a permit to engage in the advertising scheme. What advice can you give?

The Tax Problem

Your client has been found guilty of possessing property for the purpose of violating the internal revenue laws of the United States. The court found his 1984 Buick Skylark convertible to be an "active aid" in a fraudulent tax shelter scheme. Federal officers seized the car. The client does not dispute the tax fraud conviction but wants the auto returned.

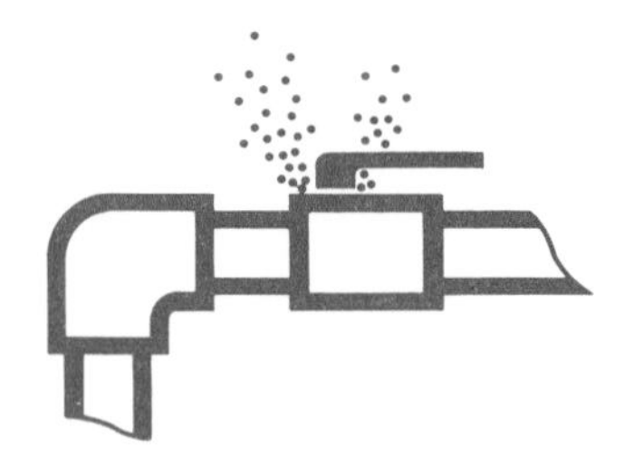

The Explosive Problem

Federal officers arrested your client for attempting to use an explosive to blow up a building used in interstate commerce. Your client allowed gas to escape from gas lines in the expectation that an explosion would occur. Does the act of allowing gas to escape constitute using an "explosive"?

The Research Process

The Threshold Questions

You will use the analytical skills that you are learning in law school in your legal research. Legal reasoning skills not only help you to determine the relevance of the materials you find, but to begin research.

You will use legal reasoning skills to begin research.

Before an attorney searches a LEXIS file or runs to a library shelf, he or she goes through a multilevel thought process that may be intimidating to the novice researcher. The attorney reviews the case file and interviews the client for facts and other information about the client's problem. Then the attorney analyzes the problem, decides what issues are involved, what action is needed, and what research must be done. For a junior associate or law clerk who receives a research assignment, the process is similar.

Experienced lawyers sometimes offer "off the cuff" advice about basic procedures and law. Without referring to any database or book, they may advise a client to pay the fine on a speeding ticket or to plead the case in traffic court. However, most legal problems are not solved so easily and require much more consideration.

The following checklist will assist you in analyzing legal problems. Use it to identify the appropriate elements and define the substance of the matter.

1. PARTIES — A legal problem does not create itself. One of the most basic questions a lawyer asks when presented with a problem is: "Who is involved?" You must identify the people, institutions, governments — even the animals or objects — that may be parties to the problem in order to evaluate and balance their relationships, duties, and rights.

Research Checklist
The Billboard Problem

1. PARTIES —
tribe state ad agency environmental groups

2. ISSUES —
Who regulates billboards close to an interstate highway but on Indian reservation?
With what regulations must a billboard on an Indian reservation comply?

3. FACTS —
Billboard / interstate / reservation / permit

4. TIME —
existing law applies
Is there a deadline for appealing permit denial?

5. JURISDICTION —
state? county? Who has jurisdiction over Indian reservation?

6. REMEDIES AND POTENTIAL LIABILITIES —
penalties if they erect billboard w/o permit?

7. ANALOGIES —
Can the state require drivers licenses on Indian reservations? Fishing licenses? Building permits?

8. COORDINATION — (do later)
need to know regs, permit requirements
find out who has jurisdiction

In the first hypothetical problem, the Billboard Problem,[1] the parties could include the Indian tribe, the state of California, the advertising agency or the environmentalists.[2]

After you identify the characters or parties, pinpoint their relationships. Are there legal involvements such as marriage, corporations, or statutory obligations that bind the parties? In continuing the analysis of the Billboard Problem, you would want to investigate the nature of the control Indians have over the governance of their reservation.

2. ISSUES — An issue is a question of law that a particular situation presents. When a client presents a problem to you, it is important to identify each issue and to note the most pertinent ones. You study the issues individually and then evaluate their relative and collective impact on the probable outcome of the case.

3

Identifying the issues is a basic task of lawyering. But it is not always possible to identify the issues before you begin your research. Sometimes research will assist you in determining the issues. If you know what area of law is involved in your case, you will have a good idea of what kind of research needs to be done. For example, the Billboard Problem involves the question of whether the state of California can regulate the use of Indian lands, which are the domain of the federal government. You may not see that issue after gathering the facts of the case. But you could become aware of the issue after you read California statutes dealing with state powers such as zoning and billboard regulations, federal statutes dealing with Indian reservations, and applicable state or federal court decisions. You also can discover the issues in cases you retrieve with LEXIS searches based on facts.

Sometimes research assists you in determining the issues.

3. FACTUAL ELEMENTS — The factual elements answer the "what" of the case at hand. What tangible objects or elements does the case involve — a house, car, computer or gun? These objects can be pivotal to a case and must be clearly understood.

For example, in the hypothetical Explosive Problem, you need to research the basic definition of "what" an explosive is. Is leaking gas an explosive?

Identifying particulars can be extremely important and calls upon your lawyering skills. In your substantive law courses, your professors often change a fact in a case, asking "Does this make a difference to the final outcome?" Sometimes it does.

Does a fact change the outcome?

Think through factual distinctions before beginning your research, even if you may not know their importance until you are well into the research. The second hypothetical problem, the Tax

---

[1]The three hypothetical problems are described on page 20.

[2]The excerpt from an Associated Press story on page 91 reveals other possible parties.

Problem, involves a 1984 Buick Skylark convertible. Is the make, Buick, important? Is the model year, 1984, important? Is the model, a convertible, important? Would you be interested in a similar case that dealt with a boat instead of a car?

In searching online, full-text databases, you search by using the words you expect the relevant documents to contain. You have the ability to search for specific facts and to change facts by changing the words of the search request. But the search you develop must be based upon a cogent analysis of the problem and your determination of "what" is important.

4. TIME — The date or time-frame of the action can be of considerable importance. Statutes of limitation govern some legal actions, setting specific periods of time during which action must begin.

The date of an action also helps guide your research. Because the law can change, it is sometimes important to know exactly what the law was when a specific action occurred. For example, tax law is subject to ever changing statutes, rules and regulations. If a tax return is disputed, the attorney considers the law in effect during the year of the questioned return. Research for the Tax Problem might require you to consider the 1985 tax laws, the year of your client's illegal actions.

5. JURISDICTION — Determining the controlling jurisdiction is a basic element of any research. Knowing the jurisdiction assists you in identifying the judicial, legislative, and administrative authorities you must consider. It also is important to note whether state, federal or international law is involved. Once you narrow the jurisdictional questions, you can choose the correct hardcopy sources and most appropriate LEXIS libraries and files.

In the Explosive Problem, the fact that your client faces a federal crime instantly informs you that you will handle the case in the federal jurisdiction. In comparison, the Billboard Problem may involve a much more complex interplay between federal and state jurisdictions. As a result, you look to both federal and state sources of law to resolve the Billboard Problem.

You must be able to describe potential remedies and liabilities so your client can decide what to do.

6. REMEDIES AND POTENTIAL LIABILITIES — Although you will not know the final remedy until a decision is rendered, it is important to know what remedies are available. At any point, you must be able to describe the potential remedies and liabilities so your client can decide what to do. Although you want to find cases which present the best outcome for your client, your advice must be based on an understanding of all the potential consequences.

It is your responsibility to anticipate problems and opportunities and to counsel your client on how to avoid or take advantage of them. In the Billboard Problem your client wants a permit to advertise on Indian lands. What are the advantages and disadvantages of erecting the billboards without a permit? Would such a course of action expose your client to penalties, or would a court eventually declare that a permit is not required? Would your client's chances for success in court be greater if the billboards were already there?

7. ANALOGIES — Are there any similar situations or circumstances you should research? For example, would cases involving boats (instead of cars) be useful to resolving the Tax Problem? You might broaden your analysis to consider cases where boats, or other forms of transportation, are "active aids" to violations of the tax laws. In the Explosive Problem, you may think of other situations that are similar to an attempt to ignite leaking gas, such as an attempt to derail a train that includes a tank car containing an explosive chemical.[3]

8. COORDINATION — When you have identified all these elements, you need to weigh them carefully so you can advise your client on the proper way to proceed. Is there one element that stands out as more important than the others? Do you have all the information you need or is more information still necessary?

After you have performed the initial analysis, you can plan the next step in your research.

3

Identifying the Sources

An attorney usually begins by identifying the areas of law that the facts invoke. He or she then identifies the sources of law which are controlling. For example, in the Explosive Problem, the attorney looks at the federal statute forbidding the criminal use of explosives. He or she also considers court opinions that construe or discuss the statute.

Legal research usually requires a combination of hard copy and computer-assisted services.

When an attorney knows the statutes and cases he or she wants to find, the next step is to identify the means to find them. You already know that a case or a statute may be found in several different sources. Often the same results can be obtained with several different tools. It is up to you to compare the results obtained with various tools and sources. Complete legal research usually requires a combination of hardcopy materials and computer-assisted services.[4]

A Brief Comparison of Indexes and Full-Text Searching

Traditional materials and computer-assisted legal research serv-

---

[3]A more detailed discussion of analogies can be found in Reusch, *The Search for Analogous Legal Authority: How to Find It When You Don't Know What You're Looking For*, 4 LEGAL REF. SERV. Q. 33 - 38 (1984).

[4]For further discussion of the interplay between computer-assisted legal research and traditional indexing, *see* Sprowl, *Legal Research and the Computer: Where the Two Paths Cross*, 15 CLEARINGHOUSE REV. 150 (1981).

ices have basic differences. For example, digests, one of the traditional tools for finding case law, are created through an editorial process that is very different from the process of creating a database.

In creating a digest, the editors start with an outline of the law, similar to the outlines you may be writing to obtain an overall view of a subject covered by a law school course. The digest outline divides broad subject areas of law into thousands of very narrow categories. Then the editors identify the legal issues in each court opinion and match the issues in the opinion to the categories in their outline. If an issue does not match with any category, the editors must consider adding a new subject category to the outline or choosing the most appropriate category in the existing outline.

When you use a digest, you identify the classification, or index term, under which you believe the editors would have listed appropriate cases.

Editors match the points of law in an opinion to a subject category.

Traditional indexes are not amenable to identifying the particulars that may or may not be important to an outcome. The editors of a digest cannot be expected to know what a later court may consider to be a critical fact. Even though a particular fact, such as a car model, can be pivotal to the case, a digest summarizes points of law instead of including specific facts.

In comparison, computer-assisted legal research services allow you to search the full text of legal authorities. The entire text of the source documents is entered into the computer. A search of the full text of opinions does not rely on a prearranged classification system or on your determination of how the editors may have categorized the issues.

Why use a full-text search? Sometimes finding cases through a digest can be very difficult if you do not correctly identify the classification used by the editors. For example, in the Billboard Problem, you might look for cases under the topic "nuisance" when an editor had placed pertinent cases under the topic "zoning."[5]

When you use an online legal database, you are searching the actual text of the documents in the library and file you have chosen. No index stands between you and the information you need. You formulate your online search based upon the words you expect a judge (or legislator or administrator) would use in discussing the issue or set of facts you are researching.

Tailor your LEXIS search requests to the issues and facts you identify through the checklist.

Searching the full text of the law requires the use of your lawyering skills. You tailor your search requests to the issues and facts you identify in going through the research checklist. What specific words did you identify as important in the checklist? For example, in the Tax Problem, if you determined that the make of the automobile was important, you might search for opinions that contain the terms "Buick" or "Skylark" rather than the generic word "automobile."

Your ability to devise a search will be only as good as your ability to analyze the problem and determine what facts and issues are important.

RESEARCH HINT

When you search for a particular fact or issue, think of the various words a court may use. "Skylark" may be too specific. What is it about your client's problem that makes the model important? Maybe there is a characteristic of that model that is legally significant.

Use synonyms in your searches. A court might use the words "car," "auto," or "motor vehicle" to describe an automobile.

Summary of the Initial Steps in the Research Process

So far we have described the reasoning process that many attorneys use to begin legal research. They study the client's problem, identify pertinent facts and issues, and decide what legal tools to use to find the law.

Often more than one approach will lead the attorney to the same result. To ensure that legal research is complete, an attorney may use several tools to confirm that he or she has found the law.

---

[5]You can overcome difficulties in foreseeing the appropriate index term or category. After you find a case with a LEXIS search, read how the digest editors classified the points of law. Their analysis may assist your efforts to find more cases.

The remainder of this chapter examines some basic concepts you need to understand in using the LEXIS service to find relevant authority.[6] Some also apply to full-text searching in WESTLAW.

Basic Elements of LEXIS Searching

Words

When you transmit a LEXIS search, the LEXIS service searches its files to find documents containing the words you have identified as pertinent to your research. It treats any consecutive string of up to 20 characters as a word. Thus, abbreviations and numerals are considered words that can be searched. For example, *7302,* a section of the Internal Revenue Code, is a searchable word in the LEXIS service.

A few words are not searchable in the LEXIS service. Words like *the* and *his* are called "noise" words. They are of such limited value in finding cases that the LEXIS service has eliminated them as search terms. Words like *and* and *or* are connectors that trigger a command to relate the words which precede and follow in the search request. Like the noise words, you cannot search most of the words that are connectors.[7]

For example, a search cannot find occurrences of the word *and* in the text of a document. To look for a specific phrase such as "search and seizure," simply enter the phrase in quotation marks, e.g.,

TRANSMIT: *"search and seizure"*

Plurals and Possessives

A search for a word in the LEXIS service automatically finds regular plural endings (that is, *-s, -es* and *-ies*) and possessive endings. For example, a search for the word *city* also finds *cities, city's, cities'* and *cities's.* If your search includes a word that has an irregular plural, you can search for both versions using the connector *OR*. For example, a search for *child* retrieves *child's* but not *children.* A possible search to find occurrences of both forms is, e.g.,

TRANSMIT: *child* OR *children*

Equivalents

The LEXIS service automatically searches for alternative spellings of certain words. For example, if you type *1st* in a LEXIS

---

[6]For a more detailed description of the mechanics of searching for words with the LEXIS service, see *Learning LEXIS: A Handbook for Modern Legal Research* and the *LEXIS/NEXIS Reference Manual.*

[7]The exception is the word *not*, which is both a searchable word and part of a connector.

search request you retrieve documents which include either *1st* or the word *first.*

However, even with this help, the burden is on you to include alternative spellings in your search requests. Treat this LEXIS capability as a backup that may find alternative spellings and abbreviations you do not include in your request.

Alternative Spellings

Keep in mind that you are searching for words as the author spelled them, not only the proper spelling. A single page of an opinion of the U.S. Supreme Court contains the word *advisor* spelled as *advisor* and as *adviser.*[8] Careful formulation of your search can prevent missing a case because of a variant spelling. Such variations can be difficult to anticipate, but you should not be overly concerned. The words you search are likely to appear more than once in relevant documents, and you have the opportunity to rephrase your LEXIS request when you see alternative spellings in retrieved materials.

Search for words as the author spelled them, not just the proper spelling.

3

Spaces and Hyphens

The LEXIS service searches for words. In general, a word is a character or string of characters delineated by spaces. When you formulate a search, treat hyphens as a space between two words. For example, the hyphenated word *time-frame* is treated in the LEXIS service as the equivalent of the phrase *time frame.* You can use the phrase *time frame* to retrieve documents that include either *time frame* or *time-frame.*

Other documents may compound the word as *timeframe.* The LEXIS service treats the compound word *timeframe* as one word and different from the two-word phrase *time frame.* To retrieve documents using either form, your search would be:

timeframe OR *time frame*

Universal Characters

Remember that the same word can appear in slightly different forms. The words *environmental* and *environmentalist* are variations of the root word *environment* and share a basic meaning. The LEXIS service has two universal characters — * and ! — to save you time and trouble in typing all possible word variations.

The Exclamation Point

The universal character "!" allows you to search for all variations of a root word. For example, using the word *administ!* in a search retrieves documents that contain the words *administer, ad-*

!

[8]The search: *advisor* AND *adviser* actually finds more than 20 cases from the U.S. Supreme Court that used both spellings.

ministration, administrative, or any other word formed on the root of *administ—.*

The exclamation point is useful, but avoid truncating words to the extent that your search finds irrelevant words. For example, a search for the word *psych!* finds psychology and psychologist, but the search also finds the words psychiatry, psychiatrist and psychic.

The Asterisk

The LEXIS service searches for the exact terms you type in a search request. If you type the word *woman* you will not retrieve documents using the word *women.* Although you could type both spellings, LEXIS provides you a convenient tool, called the asterisk.

Use of an asterisk alters the search so that any character may appear in the space occupied by the asterisk. For example, a search for *wom*n* finds occurrences of both *woman* or *women.*[9]

You also can use the asterisk at the end of a search word to limit the length of the possible word endings. For example, a search for *bank* * ** would retrieve occurrences of *bank, banking* and *banker.* But *bank* * ** will not find occurrences of *bankrupt,* which has four letters after the root.

You cannot use the asterisk to substitute for the first letter of a word and asterisks in the middle of a word must represent a letter.[10]

Remember that the basic difference between the ! and * is that the asterisk denotes a universal character for a single space and the exclamation point will retrieve words with any number of characters after the word root.

> **RESEARCH HINT**
>
> Before you transmit a search, consider the unwanted words you may find by using the asterisk and exclamation point. Do not truncate words that have the possibility of enormous variations. For example, a search for *co!* not only identifies occurrences of *co.* and *company,* but thousands of other words that begin with *co* like *court* and *codicil.*

Synonyms

As you identify the ideas and words you wish to search, consider synonyms relevant documents may contain. Remember that full-text searching retrieves the exact terms you transmit. A search for the word *car* does not find the word *automobile.*

---

[9]You should almost always use **r* to end searches for words ending in *-or* and *-er.* For example, the variant spellings of *adviser* described earlier can be found with the search for *advis*r.*

[10]Thus *judg*ment* finds *judgement* but does not find *judgment.*

For example, you will want your search for the Tax Problem to include the words "automobile," "auto," and "car." Use of synonyms can ensure that your search will take into account all the various ways a judge might express a concept or fact central to the case.

Fortunately, the English language tends naturally to redundancy and often an opinion using the word *automobile* also includes the word *car.*

Alternative Words

Words with opposite meanings often should be included as alternative expressions in search requests. A court decision on the constitutionality of a statute may use the word "unconstitutional." A decision about negligence may use the phrase "due care" to state the issue.[11]

3

A court may use "due care" to describe a negligence issue.

Connectors

Some LEXIS searches succeed by using simply one word or phrase. For example, if you want to collect court decisions that mention *golden arches*, simply enter the phrase *golden arches* as your request. In the Tax Problem, the phrase *active aid* is a term of art taken directly from case law. Organizations, such as the Central Intelligence Agency, usually are described in a phrase. However, because most legal problems are more complex, LEXIS searches can specify the relative position of words and phrases. You describe the word patterns you wish to find by using connectors.

The creators of the LEXIS service adopted a logical system of connectors to retrieve word patterns in text. WESTLAW has adopted many of them. You already use several of the most common connectors in your everyday writing and speech. The LEXIS service has only given the words more precise meanings.

The most widely used connectors are *W/n, AND,* and *OR.*

W/n

The *W/n* connector tells LEXIS to retrieve words that are found within a specified number of words of each other. You replace *n* with a number from 1 to 255. The search:

reservation W/10 *indian*

finds any document that has the word *reservation* and the word *Indian* within ten words of each other. Either word may appear first, but there must be nine or fewer intervening words.

You choose the number to use with *W/n* by deciding how closely the words normally appear. A common error is to make the number too small. Experts suggest you estimate the likely number

---

[11]A search request for the issue of negligence in the use of a pipeline may be, e.g.,
TRANSMIT: *due care* OR *negligen!* W/15 *pipeline* OR *pipe line*

of intervening words and double it. For example, if you believe that a form of the word *leak* will appear within five words of *gas,*

TRANSMIT: *leak!* W/10 *gas*

AND

AND

You are familiar with the basic grammatical use of the word AND to combine words or phrases. The LEXIS search:

indian AND *billboard*

finds documents containing both words. The connected words may be close together or far apart. The search does not retrieve a document unless it includes both the word *indian* and the word *billboard.*

OR

OR

The connector *OR* is used in searching for synonyms or alternatives. You link similar terms or words with "OR" to retrieve documents in which either or both words occur. The search:

billboards OR *outdoor advertis!*

finds documents in which there is at least one occurrence of the word *billboard* or the phrase *outdoor advertis!.*

The *OR* connector also can link concepts that are not synonyms. The search:

zoning OR *nuisance*

is a search for two words that are not synonyms but that may retrieve relevant cases. Similarly, the search

negligen! OR *due care*

is for words that are opposite in meaning, but that pertain to the same subject. Use the *OR* connector to broaden your search to account for the various ways a judge might express the issue or fact.

RESEARCH HINT

You frequently will be tempted to use a phrase that seems to fit the situation exactly. *Indian reservation* is a phrase you might initially identify as a proper search for the Billboard Problem. However, the phrase does not cover the possible wordings that convey the same concept. A search for the phrase *Indian reservation* fails to retrieve a court decision which includes the statement, "The reservation was owned by Sioux Indians."[12] Instead, consider the request

indian W/10 *reservation*

which increases the likelihood of finding relevant cases with almost no increase in the likelihood of finding irrelevant cases.

---

[12]Unless, of course, the phrase *indian reservation* occurred elsewhere in the case.

The three connectors, *W/n, AND* and *OR,* will satisfy almost all of your research needs. There are several other connectors that you can use in your searches. Although they are not used as frequently as the first three, they can be helpful in certain situations.

PRE/n

The PRE/n connector is useful when you are searching for a citation in the LEXIS service. Your search for cases that reference the cite to *Department of Transportation v. Naegele Outdoor Advertising,* 38 Cal. 3d 509 (1985) might be:

38 PRE/5 *509*

This search gives two commands. First, to retrieve all documents where the number *38* precedes *509.* The second is that no more than four searchable words can intervene between the two numbers. This minimizes the possibility of retrieving cases where the number *509* appears before *38* or where there is no relationship between the two numbers. As with the *W/n* connector, you assign the number according to how closely you expect the words or numbers to occur.

NOT W/n

If you formulate a search containing the word *reservation* with the thought of finding information dealing with Indian reservations, you still might retrieve cases concerned with *dinner reservations.*

The search *reservation* NOT W/2 *dinner* means that a case will be retrieved only if it has at least one occurrence of *reservation* without the word *dinner* in close proximity.[13]

CONNECTOR CAVEAT

Use the *NOT* connectors only when you know there is a specific problem in using the search term that cannot be corrected by requiring that additional words appear in the document. It is preferable to use search words that you know will appear and eliminate irrelevant cases by using the browsing techniques described in Chapter Four.

W/SEG

The *W/SEG* connector narrows the function that the *AND* connector defines. The *AND* connector requires that both of the linked

[13]The phrase "dinner reservation" still may occur elsewhere in the case. There is, however, at least one occurrence of *reservation* that is not within two searchable words of *dinner.* One of the few practical uses of the NOT W/n connector is to find cases containing occurrences of *RICO* (the abbreviation for Racketeer Influenced and Corrupt Organizations) without finding every case that mentions *Puerto Rico.* A search for *rico* NOT W/1 *puerto* requires that a document contain at least one occurrence of *rico* that is not adjacent to an occurrence of *puerto.*

words appear anywhere in the same document, regardless of the segment or field. *W/SEG* requires that both of the linked words appear in the same segment of the document, for example, in the majority opinion.

It often is preferable to retrieve a few more cases and use browsing techniques to eliminate the irrelevant ones.

You can use *W/SEG* if one of the search terms might appear in a segment that is not basic to your search. An example would be a search for *Indian* AND *treaty*. Such a general search could retrieve the case *Indian Head Corporation v. Smith,* even though the word *Indian* only appears in the NAME segment, and the case does not deal with Indian law. A more restrictive search is *Indian* W/SEG *treaty*. The more restrictive search is not necessarily the better search. It often is preferable to retrieve a few more cases and use browsing techniques to eliminate the irrelevant ones.

CONNECTOR CAVEAT

For completeness, this Manual includes the following two connectors, but you should be especially careful when using them.

The *NOT W/SEG* and *AND NOT* connectors may eliminate relevant documents. It is easy for the unwary to formulate a search that does not retrieve important documents because the implications of the search are not realized.

NOT W/SEG

The opposite of the W/SEG connector is NOT W/SEG. Use it with care. The search *indians* NOT W/SEG *baseball* retrieves documents with at least one segment where *indians* appears but *baseball* does not.[14]

AND NOT

Use *AND NOT* very selectively. The search *Indians* AND NOT *team* retrieves documents in which *Indians* appears but the word *team* never occurs. Such a search could miss a pertinent document that included *team* as a verb rather than as a noun with a sports connotation. The search could also eliminate a pertinent document that used the word *team* in any other context or in a footnote.

[14]Note that this search does not eliminate a case that contains occurrences of *Indians* and *baseball* if there is a single segment that contains the word *Indian* without the word *baseball*.

Combining Connectors

If your search contains several different connectors, the connectors operate in the following sequence:

The *OR* connector links words first, then the *W/n*, and the *AND* connector. The search:

minority W/10 *shareholder* OR *stockholder*

will look for *minority* within 10 words of either *shareholder* or *stockholder.*

In the Explosive Problem you must determine if leaking natural gas is considered an explosive. You could perform the following search:

1. OR
2. W/N, PRE/N
3. AND

Connectors link words in sequence

3

TRANSMIT: *defin!* OR *mean!* OR *construe* * OR *construing* W/10 *explo!* W/25 *gas!* OR *propane*

The above search requests any cases that have some form of the word *definition,*[15] or a similar expression, within ten words of some form of *explode*, and, within 25 words of any of the prior words, some form of the words *gas* or *propane.*

A pertinent case probably would cite the statute and, somewhere in the opinion, refer to exploding gas or propane. 18 U.S.C. § 844 is the section of the U.S. Code that defines explosives, so you could use the following search:

TRANSMIT: *18* W/10 *844* OR §*844* AND *gas!* OR *propane* W/30 *explo!*

This request finds cases with the words *844* or §844 within ten words of the word *18*. Somewhere else in the case some form of the word *gas* or *propane* must appear within 30 words of some form of *explode.*

---

[15]*Defin!* also finds *definite*, but you can discard these cases quickly as you browse through them. In this situation it is preferable to find a few more documents by including the broader search term rather than eliminate some potentially valuable documents with a search that is too restrictive. However, because *constru!* also finds *construction*, the search includes *construe* * or *construing* to avoid finding unwanted occurrences of *construction.*

Summary

The goal of legal research is to retrieve pertinent authorities accurately, quickly and efficiently. This chapter outlines the basic approach a lawyer takes to begin legal research. It is important to use a checklist to assist in understanding what you want to find before you begin. The checklist provides focus so you do not immerse yourself in peripheral issues. An understanding of the nuances of the LEXIS service and hardcopy sources will assist you in performing thorough and efficient research.

After defining the facts and issues that a relevant document would include, translate those concepts into a LEXIS search request. This chapter also describes how words and connectors define the word patterns you wish to find with a LEXIS search.

RELATED READINGS

M. JACOBSTEIN & R. MERSKY, FUNDAMENTALS OF LEGAL RESEARCH 9 - 11 (1987 ed.).
C. KUNZ et al., THE PROCESS OF LEGAL RESEARCH 4 - 6 (1986).
LEARNING LEXIS: A HANDBOOK FOR MODERN LEGAL RESEARCH (1988).
LEXIS/NEXIS REFERENCE MANUAL (1988).

Finding Case Law

The first three chapters of this Manual gave you background information, a foundation on which to learn how to perform legal research. This is the first chapter to concentrate on a specific form of authority or source of law.

Case law is judge-made law, the body of law found in court decisions. During your first year of law school you spend most of your classroom time analyzing and comparing cases. After law school your legal research often will begin with a survey of what courts — both in and outside your jurisdiction — have written about your issue.

The principle of stare decisis requires you to identify court decisions applicable to your issues and to your jurisdiction. Remember that relevant cases from a higher court in your jurisdiction are mandatory authority. You also can use cases from other jurisdictions as persuasive authority or to assist you in developing and understanding your client's position.

Many routes can lead to relevant cases. Case books, text books, law review articles and *A.L.R.* annotations are just a few examples of the materials you can use to find pertinent cases. Further, cases frequently cite to other cases. This chapter explains how to use the tools designed primarily to find cases.

Cases

You usually find court opinions in published volumes called reporters or in online sources such as the LEXIS libraries and files.

Unpublished and Unreported Opinions

Not all decisions are published or reported.

Most of your research will be concerned with cases in which an opinion was written and reported. But not all decisions are published or reported. Appellate court decisions have the greatest significance as precedent and therefore appellate court decisions are more likely to be reported. State trial court decisions have lesser value as precedent and generally are not included in reporters or online databases. Decisions of federal trial courts are more commonly, but not comprehensively, reported.

There can be several explanations of why a report of a case is excluded from a reporter or database. A trial court may deliver a verdict but not issue a written opinion. For example, the court may not issue a written opinion in a criminal trial in which the defendant is found "not guilty." Or, a judge may decide to seal an opinion in order to protect a witness. Court rules may give the judge the discretionary power to limit the publication and precedential value of opinions. Finally, the editors of a reporter may decide not to publish an opinion for budgetary reasons or if they believe it simply restates existing law. You usually can obtain a copy of an unreported opinion from the clerk of the court or the counsel for the parties.

Finding it All

There usually is no single reporter or online service in which all reports of case law can be found. For example, some decisions of state courts may be reported or summarized only in local legal newspapers.

Computer-assisted services usually report more decisions than are published in any one reporter series.

Computer-assisted services usually report more decisions than are published in any one reporter series. No editorial judgment is made to determine whether an opinion will be added to the LEXIS service. For example, for the years covered, the LEXIS service includes all the decisions that are published in *Tennessee Reports* as well as thousands of unpublished Tennessee Court of Appeals decisions. Every decision received from the courts is added to the LEXIS Tennessee case files.

Reported Cases

Reported cases usually are arranged by jurisdiction, court or geographic region, although online databases and some private publishers also provide subject arrangements. Because cases can be arranged in several different ways, it is important to identify which court's opinions will be most important to your research. Remember the court structure described in Chapter Two. What court opinions will be mandatory authority for your case? The answer to this question will guide you to the reporter series or online libraries you will use.

Many states and the U.S. Supreme Court either publish themselves or authorize one printer to publish reports of opinions. These authorized reports are called "official" reports. Many states and the lower federal courts have not designated an official reporter. Most courts prefer citation to official reports if they are available. Official reports usually are the last version to be published, with "unofficial" reports available during the interim.

The *United States Reports* (U.S.) is the official reporter of the Supreme Court. Virtually all Supreme Court decisions are reported. No official reporter publishes the decisions of all the federal circuit or district courts.

West Publishing Company's National Reporter System reports the three levels of federal courts — district, court of appeals and the U.S. Supreme Court — in three separate reporters. The *Federal Supplement* (F.Supp.) covers district courts, the *Federal Reporter, Second Series* (F.2d) covers circuit courts, and the *Supreme Court Reporter* (S.Ct.) is one of several unofficial reporters that covers the Supreme Court. The National Reporter System includes virtually all U.S. Supreme Court and many federal circuit court decisions. About fifteen percent of the opinions issued by federal district courts are included in the *Federal Supplement*. West also publishes three other federal reporters, two for special courts and one that covers a subject — decisions interpreting the Federal Rules.[1]

In the state courts, the National Reporter System divides the United States into seven geographic areas. Each regional reporter publishes decisions of the appellate courts of the states within the region.

The editors of the National Reporter System also add headnotes, or synopses of points of law, to each published opinion. As discussed later in this chapter, the editors arrange the headnotes in digests which serve as indexes to the National Reporter System.

The editors at Lawyers Co-operative Publishing Company take a different, more selective, approach to reporting cases. The editors of *American Law Reports* (A.L.R.) choose significant federal and state cases to publish. The opinion is followed by an extensive annotation that describes the point of law in great detail, summarizing the law and relevant cases by jurisdiction. *United States Supreme Court Reports, Lawyers' Edition* (L.Ed.), another unofficial reporter of the U.S. Supreme Court, reports Supreme Court decisions and includes annotations and other in-depth information for some.[2]

Some reporters arrange federal or state cases by subject. Examples are reporters of cases in admiralty, federal securities, state securities, and aviation law.[3]

Just as cases are published in different reporter systems, the same case can be reported in various online files. For example, a sin-

A single Ohio case construing employment law may be in several different files within the OHIO, STATES and EMPLOY libraries of the LEXIS service.

The same Ohio case may be published in several hardcopy reporters.

[1]The specialized reporter series are the *Bankruptcy Reporter* and the *Military Justice Reporter*. *Federal Rules Decisions* includes court decisions which construe the Federal Rules of Civil and Criminal Procedure, and articles on the federal courts.

[2]Use of *A.L.R.* and *L.Ed.* is discussed in Chapter Seven.

[3]Subject-matter reporters are covered in greater detail in Chapter Nine.

gle Ohio case reported in the Ohio *Official Reports* may reside in various LEXIS files of cases grouped by level of court, date, state, or subject.

Reporting the Most Recent Cases

Because of the principle of stare decisis, the most recent relevant case often will have the greatest significance to your client's position. Therefore it is important for recently-decided cases to be made available to legal researchers as soon as possible. In the past 15 years, commercial competition and the use of new technologies have dramatically decreased the amount of time it takes for new court decisions to become available.

Court opinions first appear in hard copy as individual paper publications known as slip opinions. The law library in your school may subscribe to the slip opinions for the U.S. Supreme Court and one or more federal circuits. Slip opinions are gathered in paper supplements to bound reporters, called advance sheets. Slip opinions and advance sheets traditionally have supplied the most recent decisions.

Lawyers rely on computer-assisted services to find the most recent cases.

Although this traditional method of distributing new cases still exists, lawyers usually rely on computer-assisted services to report the most recent cases. The reason? It is much faster to make a decision available in a central computer than to publish and distribute a printed version to the shelves of law libraries. For example, U.S. Supreme Court opinions usually are available on the LEXIS service and the electronic daily edition of *U.S. Law Week* within 24 to 48 hours of release. By comparison, the printed version of *U.S. Law Week* takes several days to be delivered and the advance sheets of the official reporter, *U.S. Reports*, may not be printed for many weeks after the decision.

Citation

Any time you perform research it is important to identify where you found your information. You provide a citation, which works like an address to inform others how to locate the authority.

A citation to a case reported in a book includes the volume number, the abbreviation of the title of the reporter and the page on which the opinion begins. A cite to a particular passage of the case also includes the number of the page where the passage appears.

480 U.S. 470, 479

volume number — 480
reporter — U.S.
first page — 470,
cited page — 479

480 U.S. 470, 479

LEXIS Cites are assigned to each new case added to the LEXIS service. LEXIS Cites follow a format similar to cites in printed reporters.

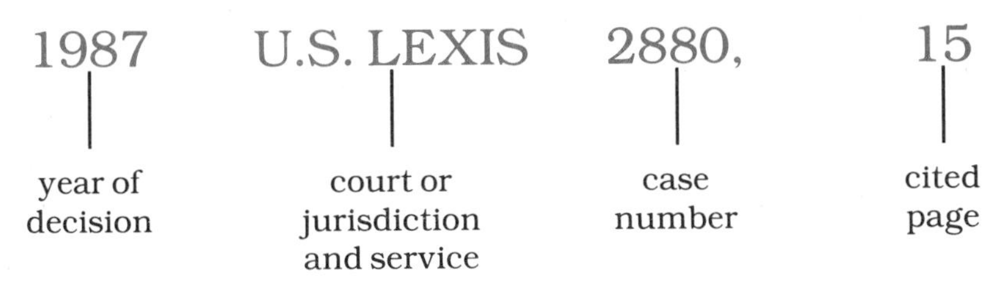

1987 U.S. LEXIS 2880, 15

LEXIS Cites are assigned to each new case added to the LEXIS service.

A LEXIS Cite is assigned to a case at the time it is made available on the LEXIS service and usually is the first permanent citation assigned to a court decision. Case numbering for each court or jurisdiction begins again at "1" each year.

The LEXIS Page is a portion of text that is roughly equivalent to a computer screen. LEXIS Pages are marked by a starred number in brackets, e.g., [* 11]. LEXIS page-numbering begins again with each opinion.

A single case that is reported in several sources has several citations, known as parallel citations. The examples above are citations to the same U.S. Supreme Court case.

Parts of an Opinion

If you have used computer databases, you may be familiar with the concept of fields, or segments. For example, in online library catalogs you can find articles by searching for words from the title in the title field or for the author's name in the author field. You can do the same types of searches in court opinions with legal databases.

Finding the opinions of a judge is virtually impossible without computer-assisted services.

By limiting a search to a segment of an opinion, an attorney can find useful information that was impractical or difficult to find before the existence of legal databases. For example, in most legal databases the name of the judge who wrote the opinion is in a separate segment. You can formulate a search to find a judge's name when it appears in that segment, thus finding the opinions written by the judge. Such information is virtually impossible to find using traditional research tools.

Before learning the techniques of limiting searches for words to segments, however, you should understand the segments themselves. Some segments, e.g., the headnotes in the WESTLAW service, may be written by editors and not by the judge.

The following are some of the elements of opinions which usually are designated as separate segments:

case name — the parties.[4]

docket number — number assigned to the case by the clerk of the court when the action is first filed. The docket number is included on all motions, memoranda and opinions filed during the case. Sometimes several opinions will be reported by the same court with the same docket number for a major case.[5]

court — the name of the court that decided the case.

prefatory action — a summary of the prior rulings in the case.

names of counsel — a list of the names of the attorneys representing the parties. Sometimes this portion also includes the names of the firms or government agencies.

judge's name — the name of the judge who wrote the majority opinion.[6] Other information that may be included in a reporter or database includes the name(s) of the judge(s) on the panel, those writing concurring or dissenting opinions, or those joining in the majority, concurring or dissenting opinion.

opinion — the text of the judge's decision. The majority opinion may be joined by one or more concurring or dissenting opinions.

The Mechanics of Finding Cases

You usually begin from one of three starting points:

1. You know the citation.
2. You know of a case, not by citations, but by the names of the parties or other unique identifying information.
3. You have issues or facts and wish to find similar cases.

1. Finding a Case When You Know the Cite — 422 U.S. 563

For bound reporters, simply go to the shelves that hold the reporter series and choose the volume by number. In the example, you would find volume 422 of the *U.S. Reports*. If the library does not have the reporter series, or, if the volume you need is missing from

---

[4]Some reporters include only the names of the first parties listed for each side. Other sources such as the LEXIS service may include all the parties listed in the original slip opinion, enabling you to find cases in which the object of your search was a party, but not necessarily a "named" party.

[5]*E.g.*, there are more than 50 reported opinions of the federal district court in *United States v. International Business Machines*, all with the same docket number. Because different courts and jurisdictions may have similar numbering systems, totally unrelated cases from different courts also can have the same docket number.

[6]The LEXIS service can search for any opinions of a specific judge or limit the search to just majority, concurring or dissenting opinions.

the shelf, check Shepard's Citation Services in the printed or online version or Auto-Cite to find parallel citations to other reporters.[7]

When you use the LEXIS service to find a case by its cite, it is not necessary to know the LEXIS library and file in which the case resides. At any point in your research you can use the LEXSEE feature to immediately retrieve the full text of a decision for which you know the cite. For example,

TRANSMIT: *lexsee 422 us 563*

You may enter either a cite to a published reporter or a LEXIS Cite.

2. Finding a Case When You Have Specific Information

Many of the research assignments you will be given will include partial information about a case.

It is easy to find a case if you know the cite. But often a lawyer does not know the cite, only other specific bits of information about a case. Many of the research assignments you will be given early in your career may only include partial information about a case. For example, you may be told that the leading case considered whether an interest in an orange grove was within the definition of a "security" under the federal securities laws. That may be all you know before you begin your research. The ability to search the full text of opinions simplifies your task, e.g.,

TRANSMIT: *orange grove* W/10 *security*

Searching based on unique pieces of information is one of the most effective uses of automated legal research. Traditional case-finding tools usually are not effective for these types of searches.

Sometimes special techniques in searching will assist you in finding a case when you have limited information. You may be assured "the leading case was in the Fifth Circuit about ten years ago and involved an orange grove. I'm sure that case will help you." The person recalling the case may remember the names of one or both of the parties, the court, the judge, or the approximate date of the decision.

You find cases in these special situations by using the unique terms and limiting your online search to the segments where the terms will appear. One search that may find the "orange grove" case is

court (5th) AND *orange* W/10 *grove*

The search requires that *5th*, or the equivalent *fifth*, be in the COURT segment. The COURT segment for a fifth circuit case typically would consist of the phrase "United States Court of Appeals for the Fifth Circuit." By limiting a search to a specific segment you often are able to find a case if you know one or more of the parties, the date of the opinion, the judge who wrote the majority opinion, concurrence or dissent, the name of the court, or the names of counsel.

---

[7]Auto-Cite and Shepard's are discussed in Chapter Eight.

Case Name — Jerry H. Summers, Petitioner-Appellee, v. Mayor Robert L. Thompson, et al., Respondents-Appellants

No. 229 — docket number

Court — Supreme Court of Tennessee

1988 Tenn. LEXIS 108 — Cite

Date of Decision — May 23, 1988, Filed; Petition for Rehearing Overruled July 18, 1988

[*1]

HAMILTON CHANCERY

Lower Court — Hon. R. Vann Owens, Chancellor.

FRANK F. DROWOTA, III, Justice, Harbison, C.J., Fones, Cooper and O'Brien, JJ., Concur.

Names of Counsel —

Jacqueline E. Schulten, Soddy-Daisy City Attorney, Chattanooga, Tennessee, W. J. Michael Cody, Attorney General and Reporter, Kevin Steiling, Assistant Attorney General, Nashville, Tennessee for Appellants.

Jerry H. Summers, Chattanooga, Tennessee, Jack R. Brown, Chattanooga, Tennessee for Appellee.

Deborah S. Swettenam, Tennessee Association of Criminal Defense Lawyers, Dickson, Tennessee, J. Anthony Farmer, Tennessee Trial Lawyers' Association, Knoxville, Tennessee for Amicus Curiae.

Judge — DROWOTA, III

OPINION

Opinion

FRANK F. DROWOTA, III, Justice.

This direct appeal raises a significant issue of Tennessee constitutional law, that is, whether certain statutes permitting a municipal judge to be terminated at will are valid. The Petitioner, Jerry H. Summers, sat as city judge for Soddy-Daisy, Hamilton County, Tennessee, for 14 years until he was summarily terminated by the Board of Commissioners of Soddy-Daisy (the Board).

NEXIS. LEXIS. NEXIS. LEXIS.

A LEXIS search for occurrences of the word *summers* in the NAME segment finds this case in the Tennessee library, e.g.,

TRANSMIT: *name (summers)*

Compare the results of searching for occurrences of *summers* anywhere in a case.

Segment searches give you important flexibility in searching. The applications are limited only by your own creativity. For example, before your interview with a judge for a clerkship you can read the judge's opinions!

There are several traditional tools for finding cases when you know unique information about the case. If you know the names of one or more parties, you can refer to the table of cases or the defendant-plaintiff table, usually located in the last volumes in a digest set. These tables have pocket parts with the most recent listings.[10] Also, Shepard's *Acts and Cases by Popular Names* can help find cases that have come to be known by other names.

Before your interview with a judge for a clerkship you can read the judge's opinions.

4

Examples of LEXIS Searches Limiting the Occurrence of Words to a Specified Segment

Situation	Sample Search
Find opinions by the late Chief Judge Friendly of the Second Circuit regarding futures contracts	writtenby (friendly) AND future W/10 contract[8]
Find cases decided in 1984 in which General Motors was a party	date is 1984 AND name (general motors)
Find dissenting opinions written by Justice Scalia	dissentby (scalia)
Find dissenting opinions by Justice Scalia that deal with the constitutionality of appointed independent counsel	dissentby (scalia) AND independent OR special W/3 counsel OR prosecutor
Find Ninth Circuit decisions since 1985 that mention Indian reservations	court (9th) AND indian W/10 reservation[9]
Find decisions in which Shaffer (or is it Schaffer?) and Heitner were parties	name (shaffer OR schaffer AND heitner)

[8]Limiting the occurrence of the word "friendly" to a segment avoids finding the many other contexts in which the word may occur. Note that a further restriction to Second Circuit opinions probably is redundant.

[9]Because the LEXIS service displays decisions in reverse chronological order, restricting the date to cases decided after 1985 probably is unnecessary. If you do wish to add the date restriction, then modify and add

AND *date aft 1985*

[10]However, a table of cases does not have entries for unpublished cases or for all the parties in a case with multiple parties. A LEXIS search limited to the NAME segment may be more comprehensive.

3. Finding Cases When You Have Issues or Facts

Digests are the traditional tools to find cases when you start with issues or facts. Digest editors write abstracts of the main points of court opinions and arrange the abstracts by subject under a detailed outline of the law. By identifying a subject, you obtain abstracts of the cases pertaining to the subject. Each abstract includes the cite of the case so you can retrieve the full opinion from the appropriate reporter. The abstracts are intended as finding tools and not as a replacement for reading the full text of the case.

Most digests are arranged like the reporters they index — by jurisdiction, court, subject or geographic region. Most of the digests you will encounter are part of the American Digest System and use Key Numbers to relate to the headnotes of cases in the National Reporter System. An alternative to the American Digest System, the *U.S. Supreme Court Reports Digest* is among the digests published by Lawyers Co-operative Publishing Company which follow the publisher's own outline of the law. It is intended for use with the *United States Supreme Court Reports, Lawyers' Edition*.

Selecting a Digest

Just as the same opinion may be reported in more than one reporter, it may be indexed and abstracted in several different digests. For example, you may find an abstract of points of law of a state case in a state digest, in the regional digest for that area, and in the *General Digest* which includes both federal and state cases from all U.S. jurisdictions.

Select a digest by deciding the coverage you want. Do you want mandatory authority for California cases? Use one or both of the digests for California law. Do you also want persuasive authority from surrounding states? Use the *Pacific Digest*. Do you want all cases from all jurisdictions? Use the *General Digest*.

Federal cases are indexed in several series of digests. The current federal digest, West's *Federal Practice Digest, 3d*, covers the federal courts from 1975 to date. Supreme Court cases also are digested by *United States Supreme Court Digest* and *United States Supreme Court Reports Digest*. Digests devoted to special topics are described in Chapter Nine.

Using a Digest

You may begin to use a digest in several ways, depending on what you know about the issue when you begin. The most common approach includes the following steps:

1. Begin with the thought process described in Chapter Three, selecting the most important elements.

2. With these elements in mind, go to the Descriptive Word Index, usually the last few volumes of a digest. Even if you are very familiar with the subject area, and know the exact topic or subject heading already, the Descriptive Word Index may suggest additional terms or theories. Use the words or phrases that describe the elements you identified in the first step to find the index terms or subjects under which the editor may have listed a relevant case.

Begin with the checklist described in Chapter Three:

1. parties
2. issues
3. facts
4. time
5. jurisdiction
6. remedies/potential liabilities
7. analogies
8. coordination

3. Go to the volume of the digest that includes your topic. Abstracts of the main points of law in cases are arranged under each topic. In the digests published by West Publishing Company, general topics are subdivided and assigned numbers. This is known as the West Key Number system. For example, "Indians" is the topic and 32(2) and 32(3) are the Key Numbers which describe points of law on the regulation of Indian reservations by states.[11] Those key numbers relate to the same subjects throughout the West digests.

4. After reading the digest summaries and noting the cites of cases that may be relevant, also read the more recent summaries in the pocket part and supplemental volumes. To further update, scan the beginning of the most recent volumes and advance sheets of the appropriate reporters for your key numbers.

Always check the pocket part.

RESEARCH HINT

There are other approaches to using digests. For example, if you already have a relevant case, note the topics and key numbers of the pertinent headnotes. Then look up the same key numbers in digests to find related cases.

5. The final step is to find and read the cases. Remember that the digests only provide abstracts of the points of law of a case. The headnotes help you find the case, not interpret what the case means to your problem. You must retrieve the full decision and read it before you make a determination of relevance.

Using the LEXIS Service to Find Cases When You Know the Issues or Facts

The following sections discuss the art of using the LEXIS service to find cases. When you know the issues or facts, search the full text of the appropriate LEXIS case files. Create a search based upon the words or phrases which are critical to your client's problem and which should appear in pertinent cases. There is no need to identify the possible topics assigned by an editor. Use your lawyering skills to determine what terms and facts are legally significant.

Use your lawyering skills to determine what terms and facts are legally significant.

---

[11]The relevant case in the Billboard Problem is indexed by two digests. The digest that is part of the American Digest System classifies the points of law under two broad topics — "Indians" and "Trade Regulation." The *California Digest of Official Reports* lists several subtopics under "Indians" and "Constitutional Law."

Almost as important as searching is the ability to browse through the retrieved cases, determining which cases to read in depth and deciding how to modify your approach to find additional cases.

Choosing a LEXIS Library and File

Just as you choose a digest, select the library and files you will search according to the jurisdiction or topic your issue concerns. Just as an opinion can be published in several hardcopy reporters, it can be located in several LEXIS libraries and files. For instance, a California state case could be found in a file of the California library, in the California file of the STATES library, or in one of the state specialized libraries defined by subject.

Creating a LEXIS Search

Begin with the thought processes described in Chapter Three, identifying important issues, facts and wording that will appear in relevant opinions. You will use these words to create the LEXIS search. Because you are searching the full text of cases on LEXIS, you can search for any word which appears in the opinion. Consider any detail that a court may find significant. Is the name of the tribe important or will the word "tribe" suffice?

List alternative words or phrases which may appear in pertinent cases. Remember you can formulate alternative expressions by using universal characters, synonyms, and antonyms. Use connectors to describe the more unique word patterns that probably would appear in a relevant case.

This case presents the issue of whether an automobile can be an active aid to an illegal tax shelter and thus subject to forfeiture under Section 7302...

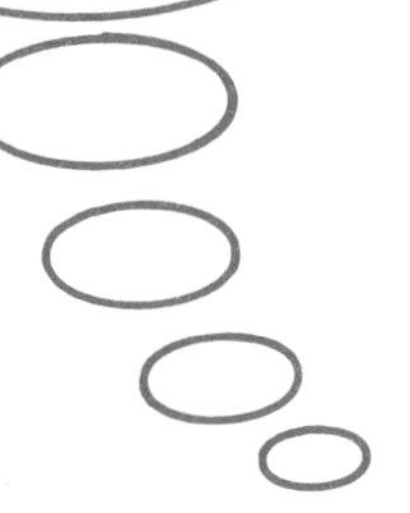

Envision the case you would like to find.

> **RESEARCH HINT**
>
> One approach to formulating a search request is to write a portion of the case you want to find. Write as you envision the judge would write. Then examine what you have written for the word or word patterns that uniquely describe the issue.

Design your search in levels. A *level* is simply a word or group of words searched at one time. The first level should include no more than one or two aspects of the search.[12]

LEXIS Browsing and Modifying — the Iterative Process

The ability of a computer to instantaneously arrange information gives you an advantage. Using traditional tools you start in the

---

[12]If any level of a search request would find a large number of documents, the LEXIS service interrupts the search to give you an opportunity to revise the search with more restrictive terms.

bound volumes and move forward in time through pocket parts and advance sheets. With the LEXIS service, groupings of retrieved cases are displayed the way a lawyer usually wants to see them — the most recent decisions of the highest court first.

Even if you retrieve a large number of cases at the first level, it usually is worthwhile to read the first few cases, since those first few will be the most likely to state current law. Also, after reading the first few cases you will know why you found so many cases with your request. The process of browsing through cases, finding citations to other relevant authorities and refining your search request is an art you will develop with practice.

Lawyers usually want to see the most recent decision of the highest court.

LEXIS Display Formats

You have several display modes for reviewing retrieved cases. In most instances, you first will look at cases in an abbreviated format to determine if the court used your search terms as you anticipated.

You press a special function key or transmit a command to choose the display mode.

KWIC (Key Word In Context) zeroes in on the search terms where they appear in each retrieved case. Your terms are highlighted in a display that includes 25 words on each side of your search terms. The KWIC display allows you to quickly evaluate how the cases use your search terms and determine if you should read the case in full. Some law schools require you to schedule LEXIS sessions so that more students can use the terminals. Printing KWIC excerpts (which include the case cites) makes it easy for you to find those portions of the cases later on the shelves or at the terminal.

VAR KWIC allows you to expand or contract the number of words which appear in the KWIC display. If you press the VAR KWIC key the LEXIS service displays 50 words on either side of your search terms. Typing a number from 1 to 999 before you press VAR KWIC narrows or enlarges the "window" of text around your terms.

... complying with the Outdoor Advertising Act. Naegele was ordered to remove all noncomplying structures. The enforcement of this judgment was stayed pending appeal.

The question we must answer on appeal is whether the Department can, through the Outdoor Advertising Act, regulate **billboards** erected on reservation land held in trust by the United States for the beneficial use of the Band. This inquiry requires us to consider several subsidiary questions.

In 1832, Chief Justice Marshall opined, with enviable clarity, that **Indian** tribes were wholly distinct nations within whose boundaries "the laws of [a State] can have no force." (Worcester v. Georgia (1832) 31 U.S. (6 Pet.) 515, 561 [8 L.Ed. ...

The KWIC display format.

RESEARCH HINT

KWIC and VAR KWIC are excellent tools to sort out the obviously irrelevant cases and to determine which cases to read in full text. To determine relevance you must read the entire case.

FULL displays the entire text of the case.

CITE lists the case names and citations for all the retrieved cases. Printing the list of cites for later review usually is an inefficient way to use the LEXIS service. Looking for the cases on the shelves and finding the context in which your search terms appear can be frustrating. If your online time is limited, use the KWIC display and the printer to determine and note the cases that are worth reading later on LEXIS or in bound reporters.[13]

Modifying — The Use of Levels

After browsing through the first few cases you have retrieved, you may want to modify your search by adding another search level to narrow the number of retrieved cases. You can modify your original request by pressing the letter *m* (for modify) and the TRANSMIT key. Each modification creates a new level of search.

You can narrow and refine a search request by adding another level.

level one: *indian* W/10 *reservation*

level two: AND *preempt!* OR *pre empt!*

Dividing searches into levels changes neither the logic nor the results of the search — a level is simply a word or group of words searched at one time. The advantage to searching in levels is tactical. The number of cases found at each level will assist you in choosing the words and word patterns that will narrow and refine the additional search levels.

There is a tactical advantage to searching in levels.

You can be more confident in your search request if you start broadly at the first level and narrow the results with later levels. You also search more efficiently than when you run search after search, each either too broad or too narrow. Many students try to pack their initial search with too many specifics which makes the search too restrictive and eliminates pertinent cases.

[13] Another LEXIS display format, called SEGMTS, allows you to select the part or segment of the case you wish to view. The SEGMTS key gives you a list of the segments contained in the retrieved cases. You then type the names of the segments you want displayed. This display mode has limited application in files of legal materials.

Starting broadly allows you to browse through recent cases to determine how you will narrow your search with subsequent modifications. You may see alternative expressions that courts use in discussing your issue. Also, terms you will need to narrow the search will be more apparent.

The goal of a LEXIS search is to describe the unique words or word patterns found in a relevant case. Yet many LEXIS search requests include too many search terms. Eliminate from your searches words and word patterns that do not really reduce the number of retrieved documents. For example, the roles of the state and federal governments in regulating activities on Indian reservations are key to resolving the Billboard Problem. Yet adding words such as *state* and *federal* to the search request does not reduce the number of retrieved cases because the words *state* and *federal* occur in almost every case.

The goal of a LEXIS search is to describe the unique words or word patterns found in a relevant case.

4

Note the words in the following search request for the Tax Problem that are not needed to narrow the result to a reasonable number of cases:

~~*internal revenue code* AND~~ *active aid*
W/10 *car* OR *automobile* ~~AND *united states* AND *tax!*~~
~~AND *federal* W/10 *officer* OR *agent*~~

Using the LEXIS Service and Digests to Find Cases

Be aware of the limitations of doing research solely in digests. As is true of many indexes, digests are slow to identify new or developing areas of law. One digest indexed cases interpreting the federal securities laws (that were enacted in the 1930's) under the topic "Licenses" for many years before creating a separate topic for "Securities". Editors categorize cases under broad topics and you should review many key numbers and several topics before determining that relevant cases will be in only one category. Reasonable people can disagree on the significant points of law in a case and the appropriate topics for each. You may think of several topics for your issue that will be quite different from the topics the digest editors have assigned.

On the other hand, you should not blithely conclude that you have found everything after one LEXIS search. Legal research is an iterative process. Read the opinions you have found for alternative terms that can be incorporated into a revised search request. When you find a case through LEXIS that you did not find through a digest, determine the reason. Maybe the case was not published or maybe it was indexed under another topic. If you find a case through a digest that you did not find through the LEXIS service, determine why your search requests did not retrieve it.

RESEARCH HINT

Keep a record of your research. Note the digest topics and the date of the pocket parts that you check. Use the printer associated with the terminal to make a copy of your LEXIS search requests. Transmitting the *r* key (for "request") displays the date, library, file, search request and the number of cases found.

Such a written record is useful to ensure that your research is thorough and to refer to when you update your research.

You also will use other tools to determine the current status of the cases you find. You cannot base your argument on a decision that has been reversed or overruled. Chapter Eight discusses the means of determining if the cases you find are still good law.

Summary

Case law is primary authority which must be considered in conducting legal research. Court opinions can be found in series of reporters or in the files of online databases. The LEXIS service has changed case law research, allowing lawyers to find cases that were simply unavailable to them by traditional means. Yet, as this chapter describes, traditional tools remain a necessary step in the research process.

This chapter also discusses the mechanics of reviewing cases. Efficient browsing, regardless of the books or services used, is an important skill. You must read cases to determine relevancy, to find citations to other authorities and to evaluate the course you have taken in your research.

RELATED READINGS

M. JACOBSTEIN & R. MERSKY, FUNDAMENTALS OF LEGAL RESEARCH 12 - 99, 430 - 438 (1987 ed.).

M. COHEN & R. BERRING, HOW TO FIND THE LAW 36 - 69, 98 - 140 (8th ed. 1983).

C. KUNZ et al., THE PROCESS OF LEGAL RESEARCH 51 - 74 (1986).

LEARNING LEXIS: A HANDBOOK FOR MODERN LEGAL RESEARCH (1988).

LEXIS/NEXIS REFERENCE MANUAL (1988).

Practice Research in Case Law

The best way to learn the mechanics of legal research is to do some research. You may try any of the examples mentioned in the text of this Manual or any of the problems described below.

In legal research there is not one correct method and you do not find one answer. Instead you often use several approaches to find several authorities that describe the law relevant to your problem. To assist you in determining that you are using research tools correctly, the problems below may be "rigged" to produce a relevant case.

1. Your client, a Wisconsin resident, has been charged with perjury. Her previous attorney advised her to lie about a savings account in a bankruptcy proceeding. In addition to defending her in the perjury action, you must advise her whether she has a right of action for damages against her attorney in the bankruptcy proceeding.

2. Your client is an antique car collector. He restored a Bugati Model X valued at more than $100,000. The Bugati was on the way to an auto show in Kansas when a car driven by a drunken driver collided with the truck transporting the Bugati. The ensuing fire destroyed the Bugati. The other driver is penniless and without insurance. However, moments before the accident, two Kansas police officers found the other driver asleep in his car in a "no parking" zone. They woke him and ordered him to drive home. The local police guidelines state that drunken persons should be taken into protective custody. Advise your client regarding his prospects for success in an action for damages against the town which employs the two officers.

3. Your client sells Luxury Cosmetics in Florida. Mrs. Smith, a prospective customer, requested a demonstration of the products in her home. Your client called Mrs. Smith to confirm the address and the appointment. Mrs. Smith told your client to ignore the "beware of bad dog" sign on the fence as the dog would be locked in the basement. But when your client entered the yard the dog attacked her. She suffered extensive injuries. Can she collect damages against Mrs. Smith, who advised her to ignore the sign?

4. You practice law in New Jersey. Your client has been charged with operating a motor vehicle while under the influence of an intoxicating liquor. He has admitted to you that he drank more than ten beers immediately before starting home on his bicycle. The result of his blood test exceeded the legal limit. Yet the law clearly states "motor vehicles" and he rode a bicycle. What do you advise?

Finding Statutory Law

5

The legal system of the United States, like the English system from which it was derived, is a mix of common law and statutory law. The number and societal impact of statutes have increased as life in the United States has become more complex and sophisticated. Today, research in the law necessarily includes the identification of any statutes which are pertinent to the problem. Statutes from the applicable jurisdiction are mandatory primary authority.[1]

This chapter describes research in statutory law. But finding a statute is just the beginning of finding the law. In order to apply the statute to a specific situation, you often will study legislative history to determine the original intent of the legislature, as well as later judicial and administrative interpretations. Although legislatures enact statutes to address specific problems or concerns, political compromises may result in laws couched in ambiguous terms. The drafters of statutory language also cannot anticipate all the possible situations in which a statute may later apply. For example, there is a federal statute prohibiting the robbery of a bank with a dangerous weapon,[2] yet the U.S. Supreme Court recently resolved the issue of whether the use of an unloaded gun in a bank robbery constitutes use of a "dangerous weapon" and thus violates the federal law.[3] The opinion cites the congressional discussion of the original bill to support the Court's interpretation of the statute.[4]

---

[1]Unless, of course, the statute or a portion of it is declared invalid by a court.

[2]18 U.S.C. § 2113(d).

[3]McLaughlin v. United States, 476 U.S. 16 (1986).

[4]*Id.* at 16.

Constitutions

Although not a statute, a constitution is the most fundamental of laws. It creates the basic relationships, powers, and responsibilities of the branches of government. Constitutions also sometimes define the basic rights of citizens. The United States Constitution warrants its own course in law school but just a few paragraphs in a legal research manual.

You can find the U.S. Constitution in several sources:

The Constitution of the United States of America: Analysis and Interpretation[5]

U.S. Code, and as separate volumes of the two annotated versions, *U.S. Code Service*[6] and *U.S. Code Annotated*

The New York Times file of the NEXIS service[7]

The U.S. Constitution is a concise document and often you will be familiar with the article or amendment relevant to your problem. Finding the relevant portion of the U.S. Constitution therefore usually does not require an index or the searching capabilities of a computer-assisted service.[8] However, there are tens of thousands of cases, articles and books that interpret the U.S. Constitution which you will need to consider. Chapters Seven and Eight describe some of the tools you can use to find materials interpreting the Constitution.

State constitutions generally are included with the state codes, both in books and online services. You can usually find the constitution in the first volumes of the state code series or as a separate file in the LEXIS library for that state. To search the California Constitution, choose the LEXIS California library. Another source is Columbia University's Legislative Drafting Fund's *Constitutions of the United States, National and State* which includes the constitutions of all 50 states as well as the federal Constitution.

---

[5]LIBRARY OF CONGRESS, CONGRESSIONAL RESEARCH SERVICE, THE CONSTITUTION OF THE UNITED STATES OF AMERICA, S. Doc. No. 92-82, 92d Cong., 2d Sess. VII (1973).

[6]There are plans to add the full text of the annotated version of the U.S. Constitution that accompanies the *U.S. Code Service* to the LEXIS service.

[7]Your school's special educational subscription to the LEXIS service may not include this file. On July 4, 1987, *The New York Times* included the full text of the U.S. Constitution as a story. To find the text of the Constitution, search for that date and a unique word in the Constitution, e.g.,

TRANSMIT: *date is july 4, 1987* AND *tranquility*

[8]A full-text search can be useful to find all occurrences of a specific word or phrase, e.g., to find any occurrences of "Indian" in the online version in *The New York Times* file,

TRANSMIT: *date is july 4, 1987* AND *tranquility* AND *indian*

To use the NEXIS service to find a specific clause of the U.S. Constitution, use a full-text search. Roman numerals are combinations of letters and treated like any other word in a LEXIS search. For example, to find the beginning of Article III in the copy of the U.S. Constitution reprinted in *The New York Times*,

TRANSMIT: *date is july 4, 1987* AND *iii*

State constitutions also usually are short documents. Therefore an online search consisting of only one or two words usually is sufficient to find the part of the constitution you need. A search that produces thousands of cases in case law files usually finds only a few parts of a constitution. The following search, which would require additional terms to limit the number of cases found in a case law file, is reasonable in most state constitutions:

TRANSMIT: *female* OR *male* OR *wom*n* OR *m*n* OR *spous!* OR *sex* OR *gender*

A search that finds thousands of cases usually finds only a few documents in a constitution.

Federal Statutes

Federal Statutes in Hardcopy Publications

Numbers are important when you are researching statutes. Remember Chapter Two discusses the process by which a bill becomes a law. When a bill is introduced, it receives an identification number which you can use to follow it through congressional action. For example, the Billboard Problem involves the *Highway Beautification Act of 1965*. The bill for that act was introduced in the Senate and assigned number S.2084 — it was the 2084th bill to be introduced in the Senate during that session of Congress. Documents that study or discuss the Senate bill use S.2084 as an identification number.

A new statute first appears as a slip law with a Public Law number denoting the Congress and the number of the law. The *Highway Beautification Act of 1965* became Public Law 89-285, denoting that the Beautification Act was the 285th act passed by the 89th Congress.

The Government Printing Office compiles the slip laws by numerical order into the official publication known as the *Statutes at Large*. The Statutes at Large citation for the Beautification Act is *79 Stat. 1028.*

Tracing the Highway Beautification Act of 1965

S. 2084
↓
P.L. 89-285
↓
79 Stat. 1028

You also can find recent federal statutes in advance sheets to the *U.S. Code Service* (discussed below) and the *United States Code Congressional and Administrative News Service*, commonly referred to as *USCCAN*. A commercial publication, the *USCCAN* contains the public laws in chronological order and publishes supplements on a monthly basis. *USCCAN* also includes selected legislative documents, like committee reports, which provide legislative history on some new laws. For the 1965 Highway Beautification Act *USCCAN* reprinted the House Report on S.2084.[9] Reading the House report gives you a little of the background surrounding President Johnson's attempt to beautify American highways and the political realities that the committee confronted.

---

[9] 1965 USCCAN 3710.

Codification of Federal Statutes

Portions of the Highway Beautification Act were changed by amendments in 1966, 1968, 1970, 1975, 1976, 1978 and 1979. Finding the net result of the congressional actions in the sources described thus far would be very difficult, time consuming, and dangerous — you might miss an important amendment.

To solve the problem of finding the most current version of federal laws, use a codified version. A code is a compilation of current laws, usually arranged by subject and divided into titles or parts. A code states the existing law so you do not have to repeat the legislative process of eliminating repealed sections and incorporating amendments.

The Government Printing Office compiles a new edition of the official *United States Code* (U.S.C.) every six years and supplements it annually. The *United States Code* arranges all federal public laws under 50 titles or main subjects.

Two commercial publishers provide unofficial editions of the federal code. *United States Code Service, Lawyers' Edition* (U.S.C.S.) and *United States Code Annotated* (U.S.C.A.) are considered "annotated codes." They have the same subject arrangement and text as the official edition, but provide you with several advantages as a researcher. Currentness, references to cases that interpret the statutes and additional editorial features make the annotated codes much more popular than the official code.

The LEXIS service contains the full text of the code as published in *U.S. Code Service* (U.S.C.S.). The information in supplements and pocket parts is combined with the information from the main volume, so the text and editorial treatment for each statutory section is in one LEXIS document.

Finding Federal Statutes

The methods you use to find federal statutes depend on the information you have when you begin. You usually begin from one of the following situations:

1. You know the citation to the section of the federal code.
2. You know specific information, such as the title in which a section is codified, a word or phrase in the statute, or the name of the original act.
3. You have an issue or fact situation.

1. Finding a Section When You Know the Cite — 23 U.S.C. § 131

For the printed versions of the federal code, simply go to the shelves that hold that set of volumes and choose the volume by the number of the title. All three sets, the *U.S.C.*, *U.S.C.S.* and *U.S.C.A.*, are organized by title and section. If the volume you need is missing from the shelf you can move to another set or to an online service.[10]

After you find the section, be certain you check for pocket parts, supplemental volumes and advance sheets. These will alert you to any changes that have occurred since the bound volume was printed.[11] Chapter Eight, on citators, discusses additional means of checking the current status of a statute.

When you use the LEXIS service to find a section of a statute it is not necessary to choose the library and file in which the statute resides. At any point in your research you can use the LEXSTAT feature to immediately review the full text of a statute if you know the cite. For Title 23, Section 131,

TRANSMIT: *lexstat 23 usc 131*

RESEARCH HINT

The LEXSTAT feature is particularly valuable if you find a reference to a statute while you are reading a case, *A.L.R.* annotation or law review article. Use the LEXSTAT feature to go immediately to the text of the statute and the editorial aids of *U.S.C.S.* After you have read or printed the statute you can return to what you were reading by transmitting

resume lexis

23 USC §131
lexstat
23 USC 131
resume
lexis
453 U.S. 490

You can retrieve the full text of a code section without "losing your place" in a case.

2. Finding a Statute When You Have Specific Information About the Statute

Just as with case law research, you sometimes begin research with bits of information — a word or phrase, a title of the U.S. Code or the name of an act.

Sometimes you begin with a word or phrase. You wish to know if there are statutory sections that contain the phrase and if there have been any judicial or administrative interpretations. For example, in the Explosive Problem the critical word is "explosive." To find the sections that use the word, whatever the context,

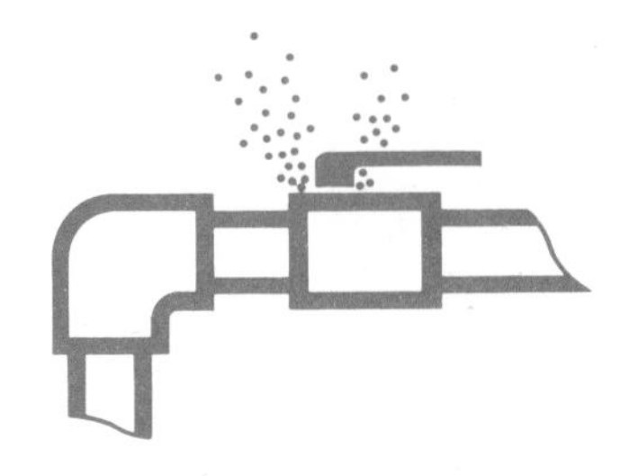

TRANSMIT: *explosive*[12]

---

[10]There are several reasons, discussed below, for using a particular set or more than one set.

[11]The publication schedule for replacement volumes can vary. The treatment of 23 U.S.C. § 131 is a good example. The bound volume of *U.S.C.S.*, published in 1983, incorporates the latest changes in the body of the text. The U.S.C.A. volume was printed in 1966, soon after the Highway Beautification Act was passed. The amendments are in the pocket part of the U.S.C.A. volume.

[12]You could broaden the search beyond occurrences of the precise word, by, e.g.,
TRANSMIT: *explod!* OR *explosive*

Sometimes you know the title and wish to find a section or sections within the title. If you definitely know which title of the code contains the sections you need, you can go directly to the topical index or table of contents for the individual title in the printed version.

For example, in the Tax Problem, you may be interested in questions of forfeiture only under the Internal Revenue Code. You could go directly to the index for Title 26, the title which contains the tax code.[13]

A special search also allows you to limit a LEXIS search to a title of the U.S. Code. The HEADING segment of each section includes the name of the title. Therefore, the search

TRANSMIT: *heading (highway)*

finds all the sections in *Title 23 — Highways*. This segment search helps eliminate code sections which may contain the terms you have identified as important, but which do not pertain to the subject area of interest. To find specific sections within the title, modify the search and add a second level, e.g.,

TRANSMIT: AND *billboard* OR *advertis!*

RESEARCH HINT

Limit your research to a title only if you are absolutely certain the sections you seek are within the title. The sections of one act might be codified in several different titles, so limiting your search to the full text or an index of a particular title presents the risk of missing pertinent law which is codified in another title.

Sometimes you know the name of the original act but do not know the titles and sections of the code in which the act appears. If you know the name of a law you can use the popular name indexes in the U.S.C.S. and U.S.C.A. annotated editions to obtain the code citations. Shepard's Citator Services publishes a volume entitled *Acts and Cases By Popular Names* which gives the citations if only the act or popular name is known for a statute. For example, if you realize the Billboard Problem may involve the Highway Beautification Act, you could look under "Highway Beautification" to find the U.S.C. cite, the Public Law number and the Statute at Large citation. If you search for the name in the LEXIS service, remember that the section which includes the name of the act may be only one of many sections in various titles under which the act is codified.

[13]There are several services, such as the Research Institute of America's *Internal Revenue Code*, that cover Title 26. Those services are described in Chapter Eight.

3. Finding a Statute When You Have an Issue or Facts

Indexes are the traditional tools used to find statutes when you start with issues or facts. All the versions of the U.S. Code have indexes, but the indexes for the two annotated editions of the federal code are more thorough than the index for the official code.

Searching the code through the index is the most common approach and requires you to identify appropriate index terms. Just as you use the digest indexes in case law research, you select possible index terms based on the elements you identified in your research checklist. For example, to find relevant sections for the Tax Problem you may check the general index of the *U.S.C.S.* under several headings, such as *Forfeitures*, which refers you to *Fines, penalties and forfeitures*. For the Explosive Problem, you find an index heading entitled *Explosives and explosions*. The annotated codes have brief descriptions of cases that have interpreted a section. Read them to decide which opinions to read.

The two annotated codes operate under different philosophies for citing cases. *U.S.C.A.* references a case if the editor of the reporter included a statutory cite in the headnote. *U.S.C.S.* is more selective in choosing cases to reference. Although *U.S.C.A.* usually references more cases, *U.S.C.S.* sometimes cites to cases not included in the U.S.C.A. annotation. To be thorough in finding cases that cite to a federal statute, use both *U.S.C.S.* and *U.S.C.A.* as well as a LEXIS search for statutory references in case law.[14]

5

The treatment of the codified version of Highway Beautification Act by the *U.S.C.S.* and *U.S.C.A.* contrasts the two commercial federal codes. Using both services you find the 1965 act and subsequent amendments codified beginning at 23 U.S.C. § 131. The *U.S.C.S.* provides the history and explanatory notes, a cite to the federal regulations which address the law, cross references to other laws, annotations in *A.L.R.*, law review articles, and three pages of court decision abstracts. The *U.S.C.A.* provides a legislative history, cross references to finding tools in the West Key Number System and eight pages of court opinion abstracts. The *U.S.C.A.* also recently began to add citations to federal regulations authorized by the statute.

Congress is gradually enacting the titles of the official code (U.S.C.) into positive law. You can find a list of enacted titles in the preface of the *U.S.C.* You must quote the law in the *Statutes at Large* if there is a conflict between the wording of a law as it appears in a title that has not been enacted by Congress and the law as it appears in the *Statutes at Large*.

---

[14]Chapter Eight describes how to use the LEXIS service to find cases, articles and annotations that cite to statutes.

Which version of the U.S. Code should you use? The unofficial codes have better indexes and refer you to other research tools offered by the same publisher. For example, *U.S.C.S.* provides cites to *American Law Reports* and *American Jurisprudence*. The annotated editions also are more up-to-date, providing pocket supplements and monthly advance sheets to assure that you have the latest amendments and court interpretations.

Given a choice between the unofficial codes, lawyers use the one with the most productive research aids for their particular problem. Because the annotated codes refer to other research tools by the same publisher, law offices often decide to purchase the *U.S.C.A.* or the *U.S.C.S.* based on their other holdings of each publisher's materials. Sometimes your choice of which code to use is simply determined by which service is available in your law library or your subscription to an online service.

Using Special Browsing Techniques on the LEXIS Service to Find Adjacent Code Sections

Codes are current statutes arranged by subject. Therefore if you find a relevant section it usually is worthwhile to browse through adjoining sections, even if those sections do not satisfy your LEXIS search. For example, the sections around 23 U.S.C. § 131 deal with other aspects of federally-funded highways. The directions for browsing through nearby sections of a code are displayed on the LEXIS screen at the beginning of each state or federal code section.

The directions for browsing through adjacent sections are at the top of the LEXIS screen.

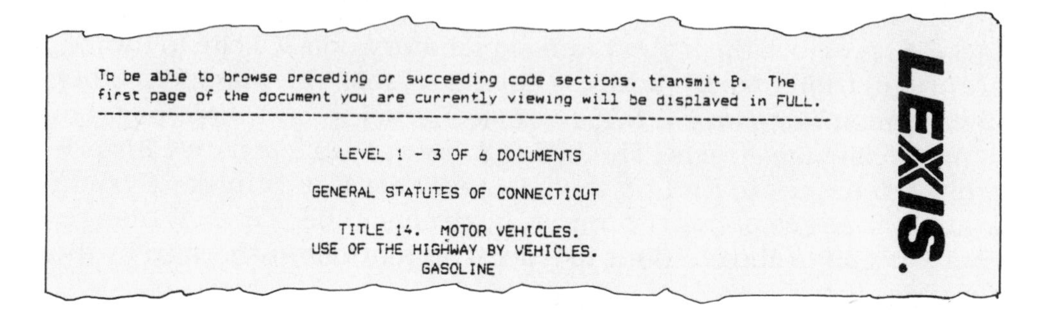

Finding the Legislative History of Federal Statutes

As you are learning in your substantive courses, different results in cases often hinge on slight variances in the wording of statutes. When a law is ambiguous or when courts disagree on its meaning or intent, refer to the legislative history of the statute.

The legislative history of a statute consists of the documents which record the bill's passage through Congress. Remember the legislative structure discussed in Chapter Two. Each step of a bill's path — from introduction to final presidential action — generates comment, discussion, and documentation. These statements are evidence of congressional intent, i.e., why the bill became law.

For example, in the Tax Problem you may want to look at the discussions about the bill that became Section 7302 of the Internal Revenue Code. Did members of Congress create the standard of "active aid" to determine if a property could be forfeited? Were automobiles specifically mentioned as examples of an "active aid" in tax fraud? If they were, your client has a difficult case to argue. In the Billboard Problem, you would search for any discussion of outdoor advertising or of Indian reservations in the legislative history of the Highway Beautification Act or its amendments.

Researching legislative history can be as easy as identifying a published compilation which gathers together all pertinent documentation or as complex as tracking down an elusive transcript of a 19th century congressional hearing. There is a growing body of compiled legislative histories for federal statutes.[15] If you cannot identify a compiled history, you will need to search for the congressional documentation created by the passage of the bill you are researching. Remember that the *United States Code Congressional and Administrative News* includes some congressional committee reports in the legislative history portion of its service.

Below is a partial list of other publications which are helpful in finding congressional intent.

Congressional Record — *The Congressional Record* covers the floor debates in both houses as part of its daily report of congressional action. The past several years are available in full text in both computer-assisted legal research services. Remember that members of Congress refer to a code section only if discussing existing statutes. You must search on the bill number, or other terms, to find discussions of proposed legislation. In the hardcopy version there is an index for each Session of Congress.

The *Congressional Record* covers the floor debates in both houses as part of its daily report of congressional action.

Committee Reports and Hearings — Committee reports and transcripts of committee hearings often are the most comprehensive sources for determining the intent of the legislators. The LEXIS service includes selected materials for a subject area in several of the LEXIS specialized law libraries.

Congressional Information Service — CIS publishes specialized microfiche and film sets that assist in finding legislative histories. Since 1970, CIS has provided the *CIS Index to Publications of Congress*. Your law library probably contains at least part of this *Index*.

[15] N. P. JOHNSON, SOURCES OF COMPILED LEGISLATIVE HISTORIES: A BIBLIOGRAPHY OF GOVERNMENT DOCUMENTS, PERIODICALS, ARTICLES AND BOOKS (1979).

State Statutory Law

State statutes share the same publication pattern as their federal counterparts. The methods of research also are similar. Because a legal problem often involves an interplay of federal and state law, do not stop your research after finding a relevant state or federal statute. For example, for the Billboard Problem you also would need to consider the California Outdoor Advertising Act, codified in the California Business and Professions Code at Section 5200.

New statutes are printed first as slip laws. Usually advance legislative services publish slip laws monthly or bimonthly while the legislature is in session. Then the new laws are published in compilations known as session laws, which are chronological arrangements of the statutes passed in a session of a state legislature.

State codes organize the current body of state laws by subject. Not every state produces an officially sanctioned code. Even in states which have official codes, many lawyers rely on commercially published codes, which usually include references to court opinions and are comparable to the federal annotated codes. The editorial features of the state codes vary. Some include the history of the section, including references to legislative history.

More than half of the state codes are available in full text on the LEXIS service and the major services have announced intentions to add the codes of all the states. Many of the state codes on LEXIS are annotated versions and provide abstracts of court decisions.

More than half of the state codes are available in full text on the LEXIS service.

As with the federal statutes, you perform research in printed state statutes and codes by using indexes. Before using a state code it is helpful to become familiar with the numbering system the state uses. Some states use titles and chapters to arrange sections by subject, while others have a straight numerical system.

In the LEXIS service use the LEXSTAT feature to retrieve a section when you know the citation. It is not necessary to choose the library and file. To find § 189.520 of the Kentucky Revised Statutes,

TRANSMIT: *lexstat krs 189.520*

Developing a LEXIS search request in a statutory file requires a somewhat different approach than in other LEXIS files. Statutory language is stilted. The texts of statutes use words with greater precision and with less redundancy than the prose of court opinions. The terms used in statutes often are not words commonly used to describe a situation. For example, "drunken driving" may be phrased throughout a code as "driving under the influence of intoxicating liquor or a controlled substance." Your LEXIS search should include both expressions, for in annotated codes the statutory language may appear in text and the colloquial expression in the case descriptions.

Use the special browsing technique to view adjacent sections in a state code. You may read words in adjacent sections that you can use in another LEXIS search.

RESEARCH HINT

If an online annotated code gives a case citation, you can use the LEXSEE feature to retrieve the full text of the opinion without losing your place in the statute. For example, the case annotations under § 189.520 of the Kentucky Revised Statutes cites 483 S.W.2d 122. To go immediately to the full text of the case,

TRANSMIT: *lexsee 483 sw2d 122*

Then, after reading or printing the opinion, return to the text of the annotated code by transmitting

resume lexis

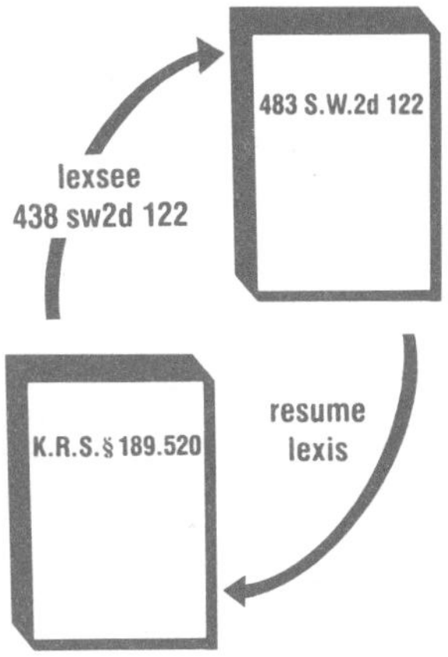

You can retrieve the full text of a case without "losing your place" in the code.

5

Finding the Legislative History of State Statutes

The legislative history of most state statutes is very difficult to research. States do not usually document, publish, or widely disseminate the debates which surround the passage of their laws. Ask the reference law librarian for assistance in finding state legislative history. Fortunately the wire services, U.P.I. and A.P., treat state legislatures as part of their "beat" and regularly file stories on the deliberations and passage of bills. Sometimes valuable information on state legislative history can be found in the archive of these files in the NEXIS service.

Court Rules

The administration of a court system is a vital and sensitive responsibility. Each jurisdiction has rules to assure the smooth and fair functioning of its courts. Although these are procedural rules, they can have a significant impact on the outcome of a case.

A part of your legal research will involve identifying the rules which you must follow to successfully present a case. You will also need to identify any available judicial interpretations of the rules.

Federal Rules

Federal court rules are codified in Title 28 of the United States Code. You can find rules and annotations in both published and online commercial codes. The LEXIS service also has several separate files that contain federal rules. Use the index to Title 28 to identify pertinent rules. West Publishing Company also publishes an annual paperback volume of the federal court rules.

There are several multi-volume treatises which provide scholarly analysis and interpretations of the rules. The traditional favorites are *Moore's Federal Practice*[16] and Wright & Miller's *Federal Practice and Procedure*.[17] *Federal Procedure: Lawyers' Edition*,[18] a newer work, is an encyclopedia on civil and criminal procedure.

Summary

Many attorneys begin their legal research with a study of applicable statutory law. If there is a pertinent statute from your jurisdiction it is primary mandatory authority and must be considered carefully.

Thorough statutory research requires you to consider the statute itself, any case law that has interpreted the statute, and sometimes the legislative history of the statute.

You can use the LEXIS service to retrieve up-to-date statutory authority if you know the citation and, more importantly, to find statutory authority no matter how it has been organized in codes or indexed by editors.

RELATED READINGS

M. JACOBSTEIN & R. MERSKY, FUNDAMENTALS OF LEGAL RESEARCH 127 - 227 (1987 ed.).
M. COHEN & R. BERRING, HOW TO FIND THE LAW 141 - 233 (1983).
C. KUNZ et al., THE PROCESS OF LEGAL RESEARCH 87 - 123 (1986).

---

[16] MOORE'S FEDERAL PRACTICE (2d ed. 1975).

[17] WRIGHT & MILLER, FEDERAL PRACTICE AND PROCEDURE. This treatise also is available on a compact disc version of WESTLAW.

[18] FEDERAL PROCEDURE: LAWYERS' EDITION (1981).

Practice Research in Statutory Law

Use both online and traditional means to gain familiarity with sources of statutory law by researching the following problems. Do not worry about constitutional issues, case law or administrative law at this stage.

1. Find Section 7302 of the Internal Revenue Code, 26 U.S.C. § 7302.

2. Does a Nevada statute prescribe the number of telephone calls one may make after being arrested and booked?

3. What are the rights of a landlord in Ohio if the landlord determines that leased premises are being used for prostitution? Can the landlord void the lease?

4. Can aliens who are mentally retarded or insane receive visas and gain admission to the United States?

5. Is horse racing allowed in Delaware on Good Friday or Easter Sunday?

6. Your client, a research institute, is planning to conduct an experiment using laboratory mice in Antarctica. Are there any restrictions on taking the mice to Antarctica?

7. Find the relevant federal statute in the Explosive Problem, described on page 20.

Finding Administrative Law

Chapters Four and Five discussed cases and statutes, two major sources of law. The third major source is administrative law, the law created by government agencies.

Administrative law affects almost every aspect of modern life, from licensing radio and TV stations to determining schedules for airlines, street parking and garbage collection. The small, rural communities of colonial America did not require sophisticated agencies or executive boards. As government, industry and life became more complex, government agencies were created.[1] Today those agencies play multiple roles — as rule maker, prosecutor and judge — and create law which you must consider.

The Federal Register and Code of Federal Regulations

The basic sources of administrative law are the rules and regulations which agencies issue. When Congress creates an agency, the enabling legislation usually includes the authority to formulate and adopt rules that will allow the agency to accomplish its purposes. The regulations can be substantive, making the statute's provisions operative, or procedural, providing practical rules for dealing with the agency. Most regulations combine procedural and substantive matters.

---

[1]Use the *United States Government Manual*, an annual publication of the U.S. Government Printing Office, to obtain background information on federal agencies. The *Manual* provides a statement of the responsibilities of each agency, organization charts and lists of key personnel by position.

A federal regulation first appears as a proposal in the daily publication entitled the *Federal Register*. You can trace the revisions that a regulation undergoes from the first proposal to the final rule by researching the *Federal Register*. The publication of the final regulation in the *Federal Register* often includes supplementary information that explains the changes between the original proposal and the final regulation. Such statements can be valuable in interpreting the regulation.

The *Federal Register* also reports on other agency regulatory actions and publishes Presidential proclamations, Executive Orders and advance notices of hearings.

The Government Printing Office publishes the *Federal Register* each day following a government work day. The full text of the *Federal Register* from July, 1980 is in the LEXIS service, usually within two to four days after publication.

Final rules and regulations are codified in the *Code of Federal Regulations* (C.F.R.). The *C.F.R.* classifies current regulations into 50 subject titles.[2] Titles are divided into parts, which are subdivided into sections. The first five titles describe the organization of the federal government. For example, Title 3 consists of all regulations that deal with the President. The remaining titles are an alphabetical list of subjects from "Agriculture" to "Wildlife and Fisheries." The *Code of Federal Regulations* is published in hard copy by the Government Printing Office and is available in full text on the LEXIS service.

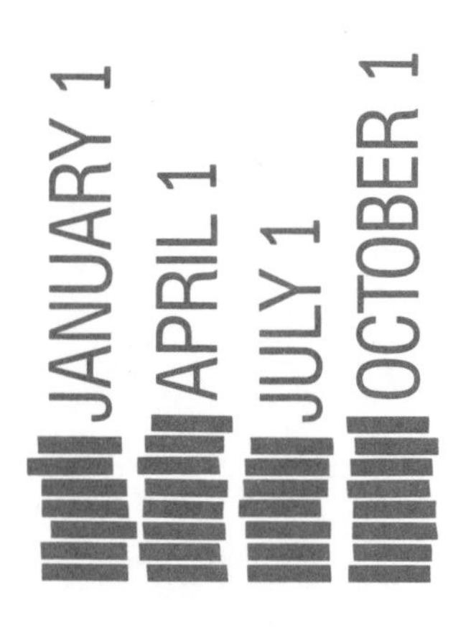

The *Code of Federal Regulations* publishes regulations in four groups as of four different days of the year.

The *C.F.R.* is compiled and printed each year. The current *C.F.R.* fills more than 150 volumes. Because of the immensity of the annual task, the Government Printing Office prints the *Code of Federal Regulations* in four groups as of four different dates of the year. Knowing the schedule makes your research in regulations easier. Titles 1 - 16 as of January 1 are printed some time after January 1, Titles 17 - 27 as of April 1 are printed after April 1, Titles 28 - 41 are as of July 1, and Titles 42 - 50 are as of October 1. Therefore the *C.F.R.* dated 1989 does not present a complete picture of changes or new regulations effective throughout 1989. Instead it presents "snapshots" of four groups of titles, each as they appeared on the days mentioned above. The LEXIS CFR file replicates the quarterly "snapshots" of the official version. Therefore the *C.F.R.*, whether printed or online, can be more than a year out of date.

---

[2]CAUTION: a common mistake is to confuse the numbering scheme of the *C.F.R.* with that of the *U.S. Code*. The titles of the regulations in the *C.F.R.* do not match the subject matter of the corresponding titles of the *U.S. Code*.

The Mechanics of Finding Federal Rules and Regulations

Due to the sheer volume and the technical nature of many regulations, expect research in administrative law to be difficult. But the difficulties are surmountable. As in any research problem, the first question to ask is, "What am I looking for?" Use the checklist for analysis described in Chapter Three.

Finding the Latest Regulation if You Know a *C.F.R.* or *Federal Register* Cite--23 C.F.R. § 750.110 or 50 F.R. 51242

To find a regulation in the *C.F.R.*, pick the paperbound volume by the title number. Using the LEXIS service is as easy. To find 23 C.F.R. § 750.110, choose the CFR file of the General Federal (GENFED) library and

TRANSMIT: *750.110*[3]

23 C.F.R. § 750.110

Finding a proposed or final rule or regulation in the *Federal Register* also is simple when you know the cite. The first number is the volume number and the second number is the page. A LEXIS search for a document in the *Federal Register* is a search for the unique elements of the cite. For example, to find 50 F.R. 51242,

TRANSMIT: *50 W/5 51242*

50 F.R. 51242

But finding the text of a regulation in the printed *C.F.R.* or LEXIS is not enough. You must determine if the regulation has been amended or withdrawn since it appeared in the *C.F.R.* You can update a *C.F.R.* section by using the monthly *List of C.F.R. Sections Affected.* The list refers you to changes since the most recent C.F.R. codification by giving you a cite to the page of the *Federal Register*.

Because the *List of C.F.R. Sections Affected* is published monthly, it is necessary to check the "List of C.F.R. Parts Affected" in the most recent days of the *Federal Register.* The "List of C.F.R. Parts Affected" in each day's *Federal Register* refers you to changes since the most recent publication of the *List of C.F.R. Sections Affected.*

There is still one more step to be certain a regulation is still valid. A federal court may have declared the regulation, or a portion of the regulation, invalid. Shepard's *Code of Federal Regulations Citations* leads you to cases interpreting federal regulations. (See Chapter Eight for a discussion of Shepard's Citations Service.)

---

[3] *750.110* is an unusual number, and unlikely to occur in many documents. If *750.110* does occur in a large number of documents, limit the search further by requiring the title number to occur in close proximity, e.g.,

TRANSMIT: *23 W/10 750.110*

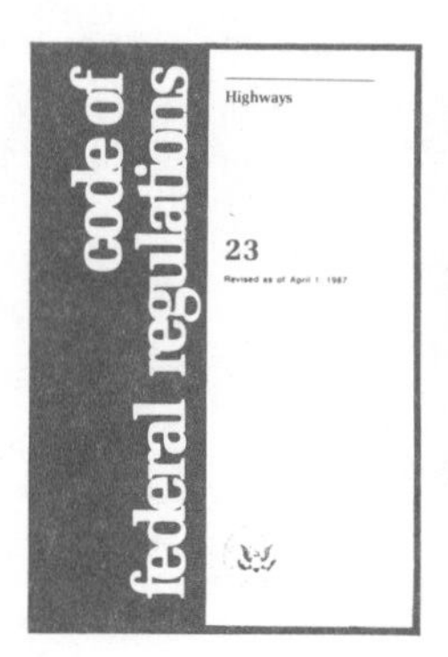

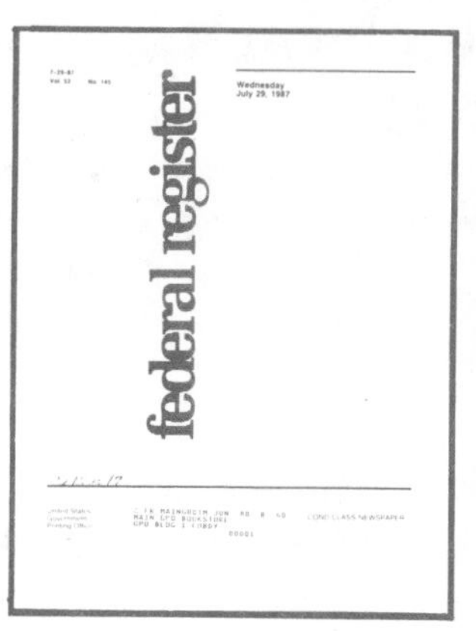

Steps in Finding the Most Current Version of a *C.F.R.* Section

Using Traditional Sources:

1. Find the section in the most recent *Code of Federal Regulations.*
2. Check the *List of CFR Sections Affected* for recent changes.
3. Check "List of C.F.R. Parts Affected" in the latest daily editions of the *Federal Register* for recent changes.
4. Check Shepard's *C.F.R. Citations* for cases that may affect the enforcement of the rule or regulation.

Using the LEXIS service:

1. Find the section in the LEXIS CFR file.

   TRANSMIT: *750.110*
2. Search for references to the section in issues of the *Federal Register* in the FEDREG file.

   TRANSMIT: *23* W/10 *750.110*
3. Search for references to the regulation in the LEXIS files of federal case law and administrative decisions.

   TRANSMIT: *23* W/10 *750.110*

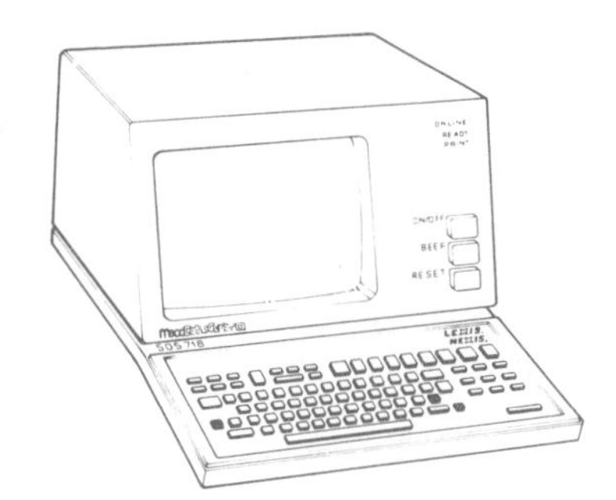

To use the LEXIS service to make certain that a rule or regulation is up to date, search for references to the C.F.R. cite in issues of the *Federal Register* published after the date of the most recent *C.F.R.* Then search for references to the regulation in the LEXIS federal case law files to determine if a court has invalidated any portion of the regulation.

RESEARCH HINT

Research in administrative materials requires checking many sources of law. Develop your own system for recording the sources you have checked. For a LEXIS search, note the date, the library and file and exact search request by transmitting *r* (for request) and making a printed record. When you use traditional tools, note the volumes, the date of the pocket parts and the index terms you checked.

```
   DATE:   OCTOBER 20, 1988
 CLIENT:   BILLBOARD PROBLEM
LIBRARY:   GENFED
   FILE:   COURTS

Your search request is:
 23 W/10 750.110

Number of DOCUMENTS found with your search request through:
   LEVEL   1...        1
```

– no cases
– 1 A.L.R. annotation

You may also want to print the KWIC display of citations of interest.

Finding a Regulation When You Know the Federal Statute — 49 USC §7401

Often you find a relevant statute and need to know if any regulations have been issued under the authority of the statute. To find regulations issued under the authority of a particular federal statute, use the "Parallel Table of Authorities and Rules" in the back of the paperbound *C.F.R. Index and Finding Aids*, the annotations after each section in the *U.S. Code Service* (U.S.C.S.)[4] or the LEXIS service.

[4]The *United States Code Annotated* (U.S.C.A.) also recently began to add references to federal regulations authorized by the statute.

6

If you use the "Parallel Table of Authorities and Rules" in the *Index*, you must update the *C.F.R.* cite by checking the "List of *C.F.R.* Sections Affected" and the other steps described above.

If you use the *U.S. Code Service* or the *U.S.C.A.*, remember to check the pocket part for recent changes.

If you use the LEXIS service, conduct a search to find references to an act or code section in the LEXIS CFR and *Federal Register* files. For example, to find references to 49 U.S.C. § 7401,

TRANSMIT: *49* W/10 *7401*

The above search will find any occurrences of *49* within ten searchable words of *7401*.[5]

Finding Federal Regulations When You Have an Issue or Fact Situation

Once again, indexes are the traditional tools for finding the law when you start with an issue or fact situation.

The index that accompanies the official *Code of Federal Regulations* is vague. For example, if you are looking for the federal regulations which limit the liability for a stolen credit card, you logically would look in the *C.F.R.* index under "credit cards." However, "credit cards" is not an index term. Nor will you find the pertinent section referenced under the general topic "credit." The index of the official *Code of Federal Regulations* uses the term "Truth in Lending" — the name of the act which applies, but not a familiar concept unless you know the substantive law of banking and credit.

Another index is the *Federal Register Index*, which is provided by the Congressional Information Service, a private publisher.

If you use the LEXIS service, you search the full text of the CFR and *Federal Register* files for words that should appear in the regulations. For example,

TRANSMIT: *credit* W/5 *card* AND *liab!* W/5 *maxim!* OR *limit!*

finds the pertinent section of the *C.F.R.* in the LEXIS CFR file even if you do not know the agency that would issue that type of regulation, the statute authorizing the legislation or the appropriate index term.

Sometimes you know the agency that would promulgate the regulation. You can use the LEXIS service to limit your search to regulations issued by a specific agency. For example, to find docu-

---

[5]Approximately 2000 regulations refer to this section of the Clean Air Act. You can limit the search to regulations in which 49 U.S.C. § 7401 is the statutory authority for the regulation by limiting the search to the AUTHORITY segment, e.g.,

TRANSMIT: *authority* (*49* W/10 *7401*)

ments in the *Federal Register* that were issued by the Department of Transportation and that mention Indian reservations,

TRANSMIT: *agency (transportation)* AND *indian* W/10 *reservation*

Similarly, you can limit a search in the CFR file to a title of the *C.F.R.*, e.g.,

TRANSMIT: *cite (23)* AND *indian* W/10 *reservation*

Finding Regulations in Effect on a Certain Date

Most research involves the search for current law and regulations. There are times you will need regulations that were in effect when an event occurred. You can find such historical regulations in the *Federal Register* and *Code of Federal Regulations*. Most academic law libraries retain both sets in either hard copy or microform.

Recall that the *C.F.R.* for any year has a "snapshot" of each regulation as it existed on only one day during that year. It does not inform you if the regulation changed during the year. To get a complete picture of the regulation for the time period in question, check both the *Federal Register* and *Code of Federal Regulations* for the year or years involved.

The *C.F.R.* back to 1981 is in the LEXIS service in separate files, enabling you to search for regulations which existed in any single year. Each LEXIS CFR file is named CFR__, with the last two digits representing the year. For example, CFR84 is the LEXIS file that contains the 1984 *Code of Federal Regulations*. The LEXIS service includes the *Federal Register* back to 1980, enabling you to check both the *CFR* and the *Federal Register* for any time period back to 1980. To see 23 C.F.R. § 750.105 on one day (the snapshot) in 1984, search the CFR84 file, e.g.,

The *C.F.R.* for 1984 provides the text of 23 C.F.R. § 750.105 as of April 1, 1984. Check the *Federal Register* to determine if the section changed during 1984.

TRANSMIT: *750.105*

Then, to find activity, if any, involving 23 C.F.R. § 750.105[6] during 1984, search the FEDREG file in LEXIS,

TRANSMIT: *date is 1984* AND *750.105*

Finding Other Federal Administrative Materials

There are more than 150 volumes of federal administrative rules and regulations in the *Code of Federal Regulations* and the

---

[6]There may be no references to 23 C.F.R. § 750.105 in the *Federal Register* in 1984. But the *750* of § 750.105 is the *Part* in the C.F.R. numbering scheme. The LEXIS service enables you to search for occurrences of all sections of Part 750 as well as § 750.105 itself by using the exclamation point, e.g.,

TRANSMIT: *date is 1984* AND *23* W/10 *750.!*

Federal Register adds a pamphlet daily, yet rules and regulations constitute a small portion of the total volume of federal administrative law. Most of the other materials flow out of the administrative functions of interpreting, enforcing and adjudicating the law. This large body of administrative law applies and develops the administrative rules and regulations.

Rules and regulations constitute a small portion of the total volume of federal administrative law.

Administrative Rulings and Decisions

Like legislators, administrators cannot anticipate the full range of circumstances that the rules and regulations they devise will eventually cover. Administrative decisions apply the rules and regulations to specific situations. Although administrative opinions do not carry the binding authority of stare decisis on later decisions, they do have significant precedential value to practitioners who research rulings and decisions to predict and influence an agency's action.

Rulings

Rulings are advisory interpretations, based on a particular situation or question. The agency usually is not bound by a ruling in later, similar situations although courts may be influenced by the opinion of the agency as expressed in the ruling.

Opinions of the U.S. Attorney General are in the LEXIS service and published in hard copy. Opinions of the state attorneys general for most of the states also are in the LEXIS service. Attorney general opinions do not have the force of law but can influence judicial, executive and administrative decisions. The number of opinions issued by an attorney general varies with the officeholder.

Perhaps the most widely known agency rulings are revenue rulings, private letter rulings and other advisory opinions issued by the Internal Revenue Service. Revenue rulings are published weekly by the I.R.S. in the *Internal Revenue Bulletin* (I.R.B.) and gathered in a bound version in the *Cumulative Bulletin* (C.B.). The LEXIS service has a special subject-matter library containing these tax materials (FEDTAX) and several companies publish tax services that include I.R.S. rulings.

Administrative Decisions

An administrative agency can fulfill a quasi-judicial role in adjudicating conflicts that arise under the purview of the agency's authority in enforcement, licensing and other matters. The government publishes reports of some administrative decisions but often the reports are published long after the decision and are poorly indexed. Private publishers and online services fill the need for public access to many, but not all, administrative decisions.

Finding Administrative Rulings and Decisions

Commercial publications reporting administrative rulings and decisions often add their own index or digest. The growth of administrative law has led to the development of "looseleaf" services as legal research tools. The term looseleaf describes the physical arrangement of the material. Published in a binder, the subscriber keeps the looseleaf service up to date by filing new pages and replacing pages containing outdated information. The typical looseleaf service is a comprehensive source for pertinent law on a subject. For example, the Bureau of National Affairs, Inc.'s[7] *Environmental Law Reporter* includes court cases, statutes and administrative materials in environmental law. The LEXIS service has similar specialized libraries that gather primary and secondary authorities in an area of law. Looseleaf services and LEXIS specialized libraries are the basic research tools for attorneys specializing in an area of administrative law. Looseleaf and subject-matter services are described in greater detail in Chapter Nine.

RESEARCH HINT

Rules and regulations read like statutes. Administrative rulings and decisions read like case law. Your LEXIS search requests should follow the same parallels. Expect more stilted language in rules and regulations. Expect fact situations and more discussion of the law in rulings and decisions.

6

Finding State Administrative Law

State administrative agencies cover a variety of areas, including the licensing of individuals and professions, tax and equalization, education, employment, unemployment benefits and other health and welfare issues. Statutes in most states require the filing and publication of administrative rules and regulations, resulting in publications similar in function to the *Federal Register* and *Code of Federal Regulations*. State administrative codes usually are printed in a looseleaf format, with new regulations printed in an official state gazette or bulletin. The indexes vary in quality and index headings are not uniform from state to state.

Research in state administrative materials can present a problem. Many agency publications and decisions are not distributed and lack indexes and other finding aids. Some annotated codes, discussed in Chapter Five, refer you to state attorney general opinions and other administrative materials related to a code section.

The LEXIS service is beginning to add state administrative codes. Other administrative materials, such as decisions of the

---

[7]The Bureau of National Affairs, Inc., is a private publisher.

public utilities commissions and insurance commissions, are available in the LEXIS state libraries and combined in state subject-matter libraries.

Summary

Administrative practice presents the researcher with a variety of sources of law beyond cases and statutes. Rules and regulations, rulings and decisions comprise the law in the specialized areas governed by administrative agencies.

Finding the relevant administrative materials may stretch your patience and your research skills. Check the *LEXIS/NEXIS Library Contents and Alphabetical List of Files* to be certain you have searched every possible file containing the administrative materials you need.

Juxtaposing the relevant state and federal administrative materials with the constitutional, statutory and case law you find on an issue will require most of your lawyering skills. Chapter Seven describes several tools that find secondary authority to assist you in finding and understanding primary authority.

RELATED READINGS

M. Jacobstein & R. Mersky, Fundamentals of Legal Research 228 - 254 (1987 ed.).

C. Kunz et al., The Process of Legal Research 167 - 197 (1986).

M. Cohen & R. Berring, How to Find the Law 331 - 374 (1983).

Practice Research in Federal Administrative Law

Use traditional and online tools to determine if a pertinent federal rule or regulation is in effect and if a revised rule or regulation has been proposed.

1. How many field laborers can a farmer employ before federal regulations require the farmer to provide toilets, portable drinking water and handwashing facilities?

2. What proposed or final federal rules and regulations deal with the Dismal Swamp Southeastern Shrew?

3. What federal agency regulates parachuting between sunset and sunrise?

4. Has the Environmental Protection Agency classified certain products as hazardous if improperly recycled?

5. A company has breweries in several locations. Must it list the addresses of all the breweries or just the principal place of business of the brewer on the label of each can of beer?

6. Must flight attendants remain on the plane during intermediate stops?

Finding Secondary Authority and Non-Legal Materials

Final appellate decisions, statutes and regulations are the main sources of primary authority. But, as this chapter describes, in the practice of law you often need to find more than primary authorities.

To understand a legal issue, you may need to know about current lawsuits, settlements, appeals, enforcement actions and proposed legislation that are not covered by the sources discussed so far in this Manual. You also may need assistance finding and understanding particularly complex issues of substantive and procedural law. Fact situations may require knowledge of complex technologies or industries. The first part of this chapter describes how to find secondary authorities that can assist in finding and understanding the law. The second part describes how to find non-legal information to use in the practice of law.

Finding Secondary Authority

Sometimes you do not know where to start. You may be concerned that you do not have sufficient background in an area of law. You may have difficulty finding primary authorities. You may worry that you have not thought of all the approaches or arguments related to your client's problem. When faced with such situations, turn to secondary authorities.

Developing areas of law generally have little or no primary authority because courts or legislatures have not yet addressed many of the issues. Again, you may turn to secondary authorities.

Secondary authority assists you in finding and understanding primary authority, an area of law or an approach to a legal problem.[1]

Fundamental Descriptions of Law — Dictionaries and Encyclopedias

The most basic secondary materials are legal dictionaries and encyclopedias.

You probably already have purchased a legal dictionary and know that the interpretation of a word can determine the outcome of a case. The most widely used dictionaries are *Black's*, available in hard copy or on WESTLAW, and *Ballantine's*.[2]

Often you need to find how terms are used in primary authorities. You can use *Words and Phrases*, a multi-volume set, or the LEXIS service to find definitions of terms in primary authorities. LEXIS users have developed several variations of a search to find words defined in primary authorities. If you believe the term will appear rarely in a LEXIS file, simply search for the word or phrase. For example,

TRANSMIT: *active ingredient*

If you believe the term will appear many times in a LEXIS file, envision the words that would be likely to appear in close proximity to the defined word or phrase. For example,

TRANSMIT: *active ingredient* W/10 *define** OR
definition OR *mean!* OR
*constru**** OR *interpret!*

Encyclopedias are helpful when you need a beginning outline and summary of the law. Legal encyclopedias give you a general statement of an area of law — "black letter" law — and provide a means to find applicable cases and statutes. The two leading encyclopedias are *American Jurisprudence, Second Series* (Am.Jur.2d) and *Corpus Juris Secundum* (C.J.S.). Both provide organized statements of law in a logical outline. Although both cite to cases and statutes, the editors of *Am.Jur.2d* cite to cases on a more selective basis, choosing controlling cases that interpret and construe the law.

Legal Treatises

Legal treatises provide extensive analyses of an area of law. The authors of treatises are attorneys, often law professors, who have practiced or taught in a subject. Treatises can be a single volume, e.g., *Psychiatric Evidence*, or a multi-volume set, e.g., *American*

---

[1] Looseleaf services, which often combine primary and secondary authorities on a topic in a single source, are described in Chapter Nine.

[2] A more recently published dictionary is B.A. GARNER, A DICTIONARY OF MODERN LEGAL USAGE (1987).

Law of Products Liability, 3d. While treatises are very helpful and easy to use, lawyers who need them often are unaware they exist. Check your law library catalog, look at the office shelves of an attorney or faculty member who specializes in that area of law, or note references to treatises in cases that you find. Many treatises, such as Wright & Miller's *Civil Practice and Procedure* and *Moore's Federal Practice*, are cited frequently by courts.[3]

Legal Periodicals

Legal periodicals fill a wide range of information needs for lawyers.

Legal periodicals fill a wide range of information needs for lawyers.

Local legal newspapers, e.g., *New York Law Journal*, cover local court activity. Some periodicals, e.g., *Journal of The American Bar Association* and *National Law Journal*, provide more general articles on the practice of law. Scholarly analyses and comment are provided by some subject-oriented periodicals, e.g., *The Business Lawyer*, and by student-edited law reviews, e.g., *Michigan Law Review*.

Law reviews contain several different types of articles which may in turn be given different weight by courts. Articles may be written by practitioners, professors or even judges. Articles often go beyond descriptions of the law to offer critical, evaluative commentary or thought-provoking proposals. If the author is recognized as an expert in the area, his or her statements can provide persuasive authority. Law reviews also include notes and comments written by students that provide scholarly treatment of a case or subject. Such notes and comments assist you in understanding or finding the law. Finally, law reviews may also have book reviews of treatises or other law books.

Some Types of Legal Periodicals:

- **Legal newspapers**
- **Bar journals**
- **Law reviews**
- **Newsletters**

Some newsletters offer assistance to lawyers who practice in a special area of law. For example, *Hospital Vigil*, published by The Association of Hospital Attorneys, provides coverage of ongoing litigation and recent decisions in the field of health law. *Tax Notes Today* provides exhaustive coverage of tax developments each day. *Middle East Executive Reports* is written for lawyers and their clients who do business in that area of the world.

Some highly specialized newsletters cover a single legal action, often a major bankruptcy or class action suit, that involves many lawyers and parties. Such newsletters keep interested parties up to date on the litigation, then cease publication after the lawsuits are settled.

7

---

[3] You can use the LEXIS service to go from an oft-cited treatise to recent cases that cite the treatise. For example, to find cases citing Paragraph 9.12 of *Moore's Federal Practice*, choose a LEXIS case law file and

TRANSMIT: *moore* W/10 *9.12* OR *p9.12*

(Paragraph symbols (¶) are entered as the letter *p* in the LEXIS service so the word *p9.12* in a LEXIS search retrieves ¶9.12 in the original text.)

Many specialty newsletters have limited circulation and some are expensive. Some are only available electronically. Some are not found in most law libraries. Yet they can be invaluable to an attorney with an interest in a special area of law.

How to Find Articles in Legal Periodicals

Periodicals are indexed by the *Index to Legal Periodicals, Current Law Index* and *Legal Resource Index*. All are available in a variety of media — do not hesitate to ask the librarian — and are easy to use.

The LEXIS service enables you to find articles in legal periodicals using both the indexes and searches of the full text of the articles. Why does LEXIS have both indexes and the full text? One reason is that coverage varies. Sometimes indexes cover more journals and go back further in time. Sometimes the license to include a journal in the LEXIS service does not cover every article. On the other hand, the LEXIS service sometimes includes articles or entire periodicals that indexes do not cover. Finally, searching the full text of legal periodicals enables you to find articles on points that may not be indexed. Thorough researchers search both the indexes and the full-text files of legal periodicals in the LEXIS service.

RESEARCH HINT

Index entries are brief but divided into several segments. It is best to use a broad LEXIS search in files of indexes, e.g.,

TRANSMIT: *enjoin!* OR *injunction* AND *environment!* OR *pollut!*

Search the full text of law reviews for tighter patterns of words, using the same search techniques that you use in searches of case law, e.g.,

TRANSMIT: *enjoin!* OR *injunction* W/15 *environment!* OR *pollut!*

Most of the legal periodicals in the LEXIS service are included in full text in the Law Review (LAWREV) library. However, you should consult the *LEXIS/NEXIS Library Contents* because the indexes and full text of several journals are included elsewhere in specialized LEXIS libraries and the NEXIS service. Several publications in the NEXIS service, notably the *American Banker*, *Daily Report for Executives* and *Foster's Natural Gas Report*, include extensive coverage of administrative law.

American Law Reports and *Lawyers' Edition* Annotations

Imagine up-to-date law review articles on 13,000 subjects and you have the nuclei of *American Law Reports* (A.L.R.). A thorough, thoughtful analysis of a point of law, an annotation organizes and explains a specific topic in detail. *A.L.R.* annotations frequently are cited by courts. Reading an annotation can be an excellent way to begin research.

A.L.R. includes both reports of cases (primary authority) and editorial analysis (secondary authority). Chapter Four describes *A.L.R.* as a reporter of selected cases. The editors of *A.L.R.* choose appellate decisions of state and federal courts, decisions they believe have wide significance. The opinions are reported in *American Law Reports* and followed by an exhaustive analysis of the holding of the case. The analysis is called the annotation.

Yet *A.L.R.* annotations probably have been underutilized in the past because they were difficult to find. It is now much easier to identify relevant annotations because the indexes have improved, the full text of *A.L.R.* is on the LEXIS service, and you can find references to relevant *A.L.R.* annotations by using citator services such as Auto-Cite.

Chapter Four describes the annotated reporter titled *United States Supreme Court Reports, Lawyers' Edition* (L.Ed.). The last portion of each volume of *L.Ed.* also includes detailed articles, or annotations, on the main point of law in several of the U.S. Supreme Court cases reported in that volume.

The printed version of *A.L.R.* includes both the reports of significant cases and the annotations. The ALR file in the LEXIS service includes only the annotations.

_A.L.R._ and _L.Ed._ 2d series in the LEXIS service

A.L.R.2d	100 volumes of annotations written from 1948 through 1965 and updated annually
A.L.R.3d	100 volumes of annotations written from 1965 through 1980 and updated annually
A.L.R.4th	annotations written from 1980 to date and updated annually
A.L.R.Fed.	annotations on issues from federal courts written from 1969 to date and updated annually
L.Ed.2d	annotations and summaries of briefs for selected U.S. Supreme Court decisions from volume 350 U.S. that are updated annually

The annotations of the A.L.R. and L.Ed. 2d series listed in the box are combined into one file in the LEXIS service. You can search them all with a single search.

Finding Cases and Annotations in *A.L.R.* and *L.Ed.*

A new "Index to Annotations" — which covers the hardcopy *A.L.R.2d, A.L.R.3d, A.L.R.4th, A.L.R. Federal* and *L.Ed.2d* — has made finding an annotation considerably easier. There is a "Quick Index" to the first, and oldest, series of annotations (which are neither updated in the same manner as the later series nor included in the LEXIS service). There are individual digests for *A.L.R.* (first series) and *A.L.R.2d*, and a combined digest for *A.L.R.3d*, *A.L.R.4th*, *A.L.R. Fed.* and *L.Ed.2d*. The digests arrange the annotations by subject and present a short summary of the reported decisions. Be certain to check the pocket parts of the *A.L.R.* indexes and digests.

You also can search the full text of *A.L.R.* annotations in the LEXIS service. All of the *A.L.R.* and *L.Ed.2d* annotations in the LEXIS service are combined in a single file — ANNO — so all can be searched at one time.

RESEARCH HINT

The ANNO file of the LEXIS service contains the *A.L.R.* annotations and not the related court opinions. However, you can search both court opinions and *A.L.R.* annotations at the same time by searching one of the large, combined case law files, e.g., GENFED COURTS or STATES OMNI. The results of your search are grouped — cases in Group 1 and annotations in Group 2. You can display the retrieved documents from either group and move from one group to another at any time.

Features of *A.L.R.* and *L.Ed.* in Print and on the LEXIS Service

Case — The printed version of *A.L.R.* includes the full text of the case that illustrates the point of law under consideration in the annotation. The LEXIS version does not include the case in the ANNO file since it is reported elsewhere in the LEXIS libraries.

Cross-References — The cross-references point you to the same point of law in other legal publications produced by the publisher.

Table of Contents — Because annotations can be many LEXIS screens, all but the shortest annotations have tables of contents. The table of contents can assist you in identifying specific issues without reading the entire annotation.[4]

Alphabetical Word Index — Most annotations have an index of persons, places, objects, acts and legal concepts mentioned in the annotation.[5]

---

[4]Because an A.L.R. annotation can be lengthy, the LEXIS version enables you to immediately move from the table of contents to view the full-text of a section. Type the term *p∗* followed by the section number. For example, to see Section 5 without paging through the document,

TRANSMIT: *p∗5*.

[5]Transmit *p∗index* to display the index without paging through the annotation. See footnote 4 for instructions on displaying a particular section.

Table of Jurisdictions Represented — This table lists the jurisdiction whose cases are discussed or cited within the annotation. The table enables you to locate quickly the cases most pertinent to your jurisdiction. In the *ALR Federal* series, it is called the "Tables of Contents and Circuits." *A.L.R.* annotations on the LEXIS service also contain a "Table of Cases" which lists by jurisdiction all cases cited in the annotation.

Annotation — The text of the annotation is the core of *A.L.R.* Under a topical outline, it discusses cases on the subject of the annotation. The text also includes several prefatory portions which can be helpful to the researcher. The "Related Matters" portion leads you directly to other annotations, textbooks, treatises and law review articles on closely related topics. "Practice Pointers" provides practical and procedural approaches when dealing with the subject of the annotation. Typically this portion gives you suggestions on how to plead, prepare the brief, present evidence or draft a document.

How To Bring Your Research in *A.L.R.* and *L.Ed. 2d* Up to Date

Annual cumulative supplements discuss changes in the law and analyze the impact of new cases. The supplements are pocket parts kept inside the back cover of bound volumes. Always check the pocket part to see if any sections of an annotation have been updated.

The online version of *A.L.R.* on the LEXIS service is updated with the same annual cumulative supplements at the same time the printed version is published. But, instead of one supplement for each volume, the supplemental information in the online version is added to the end of each affected section of an annotation. Your LEXIS search finds occurrences of words in both the original text and the supplement. Thus, you need no reminder and expend no extra effort to search or read the supplement in the LEXIS version.

Records and Briefs

A case may so closely match your problem that you simply must find more about it than is revealed in the reported opinion. You may want to talk to the counsel for the parties or review the other documents that constitute the court record. Why? One reason is to obtain a better understanding of the arguments of counsel. You also may find facts that were not mentioned in the opinion and are valuable because they relate to the decision or because the information is not available anywhere else.

Court records document a lawsuit. The record can include the original complaint, motions and pleadings, the transcript of the proceedings, jury instructions and other documents. Particularly at the appellate level, attorneys for both sides write briefs of the case for the court to consider. Briefs restate the facts, analyze the law and present the legal arguments.

Finding briefs and court records can be difficult. You can call or write the clerk of the court to obtain a copy, identify a law library that has briefs as part of its collection, or call or write the counsel. Some academic law libraries have federal circuit court briefs on microfiche, and most law libraries have U.S. Supreme Court records and briefs.

Seach for references to cases, statutes, legal principles or names in the LEXIS Supreme Court briefs (BRIEFS) file.

The full text of U.S. Supreme Court briefs (for cases that are scheduled for argument) are in a file of the LEXIS service. The ability to search the full text of briefs for any reference to a case, statute, principle or name increases the ways you can use briefs of prior cases in your practice.

State Filings

All states require, usually through state statute, organizations doing business within the state to file certain information about the business with a state authority, often the department of commerce or state secretary of state. The information contained in the filings usually includes the name and address of the corporation or partnership and the articles of incorporation. The content of the filings is neither primary nor secondary authority as described by this Manual, but this information is very important to a lawyer. If you sue a corporation you must use the correct name on the complaint. Even more important is the registered agent for service of process if you sue an out-of-state corporation.

Certain debts that are secured with personal property, such as inventory, equipment and accounts receivable, are recorded by filing with state or local authorities. The information in these filings, generally called Uniform Commercial Code filings, and the rights they give the lender, also are important to a lawyer.

The process of obtaining information from state filings is undergoing a dramatic change. In all states, you obtain filing information by calling or writing the state agency or engaging a company that specializes in such matters.[6] Now in several states commercial services make the information filed with the state agency available for search and retrieval. The INCORP materials in the LEXIS service contain selected filing information for several states. Find the information you need by using a search as you would in any other LEXIS file.

---

[6]You can obtain copies of records and submit filings on your clients' behalf through several private services, including the LEXIS document services.

Finding Non-Legal Materials

One hundred years ago a judge riding circuit needed only a rudimentary knowledge of agriculture and mechanics to complement the law books in his saddlebag. Today an attorney must quickly be facile with subjects such as electronic fund transfers, polymers and herniated disks. This section describes how attorneys use a broad range of non-legal sources to find the information they need to fulfill their professional responsibilities.

As an attorney, you need to gauge the attitudes and positions of people responsible for making, enforcing and interpreting the law. Your client may face a drunk driving charge and you must anticipate the actions of the prosecutor and judge. Or, your client may be considering the acquisition of a competitor and you must predict the reactions of the staff and Commissioners of the Federal Trade Commission. Business clients in particular need to know of proposed laws and regulations, whether in tax, trade, or zoning, in order to plan.

As an attorney you need information to assist you in preparing for trial. As you know, neither the current status nor the results of every lawsuit and enforcement action can be found in most reported primary authority. Often reports of litigations and settlements are included in newspapers and wire stories. Have the judge, parties or counsel involved in your matter been in the news lately? Having such information may affect the advice you give your client. You may need to find and evaluate experts, obtain background information on factual issues and find non-legal authority for the arguments or facts you will present. You may need to know how beer is brewed, how tests determine the presence of drugs in humans or how advertising agencies measure the effectiveness of billboards.

Often reports of litigations and settlements are included in newspapers and wire stories.

How can an attorney be knowledgeable in all these areas? Today attorneys depend on more than client conferences and pre-trial discovery to understand the facts of a problem. Included with most subscriptions[7] to the LEXIS service are several services offering news, financial, medical and other "non-legal" information that is definitely related to legal practice. The NEXIS news and business information service and related services have become major resources for attorneys. This section describes how attorneys use the NEXIS and related services in their practices.

[7]Subscription agreements for law schools may limit the availability of the NEXIS and related services to law students.

NEXIS and Related Services

The NEXIS service includes more than 350 sources of general news and business information. The NEXIS service applies the same basic concept as the LEXIS service: you formulate searches for occurrences of words and word patterns in the full text of documents. You may search broad group files containing collections of newspapers, magazines, newsletters or wire services, or individual files of single titles such as *Business Week* or *The New York Times*. You may recognize many of the publications and wire services in the NEXIS service. Some, such as *Engineering News Record* and *Business Insurance*, probably are less familiar. The NEXIS publications assist attorneys in finding useful information published in a wide range of subjects from yesterday to as many as 15 years ago.

Courts often cite newspapers and magazines as authority for certain facts. Because of its reputation for consistent, high-quality reporting and its policy of correcting even slight copy errors in later editions,[8] *The New York Times* is one of the most frequently cited non-legal sources of information.

The library of financial and company information (COMPNY) includes the full text of government-required filings as well as the full text of research reports on companies and industries by Wall Street analysts. The library also has databases of company information that can be searched to find companies in a certain industry, of a certain size or another characteristic.

The NAARS library includes portions of company annual reports to shareholders as well as authoritative literature on accounting rules and practices. Other non-legal materials include a file of abstracts of articles from publications of general interest and an extensive library of medical literature that includes an online index.

Using the NEXIS and Related Services

The search techniques for the NEXIS service are the same as for the LEXIS service, but you should avoid searching for legal terms and citations that are more likely to be used in primary and secondary legal authorities. For example, as part of the preparation for the Tax Problem, you may want to know if the I.R.S. recently has seized cars involved in other fraudulent tax shelters. It is unlikely that a news report or article will refer to Section 7302 of the Internal Revenue Code or the court-defined standard of an "active aid." A more likely word pattern for a general-interest publication might be, e.g.,

TRANSMIT: *car* OR *auto* OR *automobile* W/25
tax W/3 *shelter*

---

[8]Corrections are electronically "stitched" to the original story in the NEXIS version, thereby alleviating the concern that you might miss a correction printed on a later date.

If the preceding search retrieves a large number of stories, you could add a second level requiring that additional words occur in close proximity, e.g.,

TRANSMIT: W/10 *illegal!* OR *fraud!*

The practical uses of the NEXIS and related services are limited only by your creativity. For example, unreported cases, pending lawsuits and settlements may be described only in newspaper, magazine or wire stories. When a major lawsuit commences or settles, the parties often issue press releases which may be the only publicly available account of the litigation. A search through the NEXIS files of business stories and press releases may give you that information. The following excerpt from an Associated Press story relates a development and background information in the case that is the basis of the Billboard Problem.

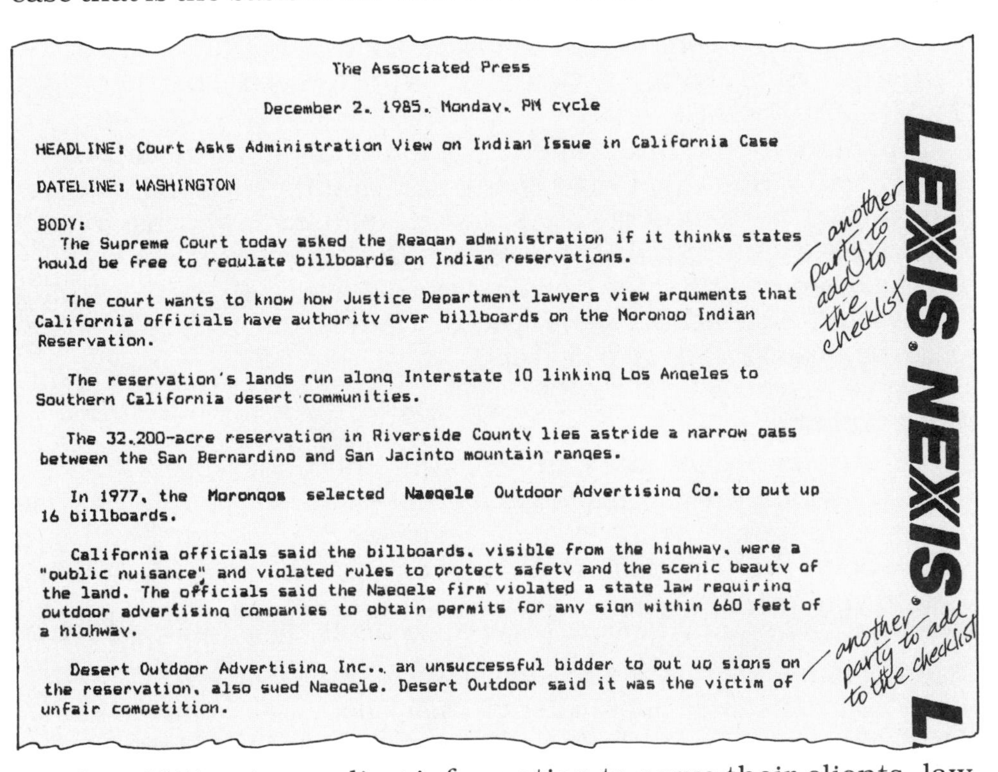

The Associated Press

December 2, 1985, Monday, PM cycle

HEADLINE: Court Asks Administration View on Indian Issue in California Case

DATELINE: WASHINGTON

BODY:
The Supreme Court today asked the Reagan administration if it thinks states hould be free to regulate billboards on Indian reservations.

The court wants to know how Justice Department lawyers view arguments that California officials have authority over billboards on the Morongo Indian Reservation.

The reservation's lands run along Interstate 10 linking Los Angeles to Southern California desert communities.

The 32,200-acre reservation in Riverside County lies astride a narrow pass between the San Bernardino and San Jacinto mountain ranges.

In 1977, the **Morongos** selected **Naegele** Outdoor Advertising Co. to put up 16 billboards.

California officials said the billboards, visible from the highway, were a "public nuisance" and violated rules to protect safety and the scenic beauty of the land. The officials said the Naegele firm violated a state law requiring outdoor advertising companies to obtain permits for any sign within 660 feet of a highway.

Desert Outdoor Advertising, Inc., an unsuccessful bidder to put up signs on the reservation, also sued Naegele. Desert Outdoor said it was the victim of unfair competition.

In addition to needing information to serve their clients, law firms are businesses with the information needs of any other business. They are interested in obtaining new clients, client development, knowing how the media describes their firm and the activities of other law firms. The NEXIS service assists firms in learning more about clients and prospective clients, other law firms and themselves.[9] As a law student, you may search for news accounts

[9]To facilitate finding news accounts of clients, etc., that might otherwise be missed, firms often set up a NEXIS search that runs automatically at regular intervals. This feature, called the ECLIPSE feature, provides regular reports of the latest results of the search.

of government agencies, corporate legal departments or firms that are potential employers.

Lawyers frequently need the assistance of an expert who can brief them on a topic or appear as a witness. A NEXIS search for an expert includes terms that denote that one is an authority on a subject, e.g.,

TRANSMIT: *dr* OR *doctor!* OR *professor* OR *expert!* OR *authority* W/10 *polymer*[10]

A NEXIS search can sometimes provide interesting information on opposing parties, witnesses and experts.

Dialog Information Retrieval Service

Another database service that is popular among attorneys is the DIALOG Information Retrieval Service. DIALOG includes hundreds of databases on a wide variety of subjects. Of particular interest to attorneys are the *Legal Resource Index,* CIS (CONGRESSIONAL INFORMATION SERVICE), *Congressional Record* Abstracts and TRADEMARKSCAN.

As many of the titles reflect, the materials in these databases are abstracts. Since they are not full text, you must use appropriate indexing terms in most of your searches. In many law firms, trained librarians search the DIALOG service. But as attorneys in smaller firms also are realizing the benefit of the databases, they are learning to use DIALOG. DIALOG offers special seminars that survey the databases of greatest interest to lawyers.

Summary

Secondary materials help you find and understand the law. You can waste time, miss ideas and lose cases if you do not use them. A danger in using secondary authorities is relying on them to the point that you do not carefully analyze the primary authorities on your own.

After you graduate from law school, you will spend more time reading non-legal materials -- newspapers, magazines and newsletters -- to be informed about clients, their business and news that affects your practice. At times you may need a piece of information you recall reading, but you have forgotten the source. Because the NEXIS and related services are readily accessible and use the same searching techniques as the LEXIS service, they can be a ready source of non-legal information. The ability to search for any name, word or word pattern in the NEXIS service gives you the ability to pursue information on any idea.

---

[10]The LEXIS service also has a directory of experts listed by area of expertise. To search the directory, drop the other search terms and simply search for occurrences of the specialty, e.g.,

TRANSMIT: *polymers*

RELATED READINGS

M. COHEN & R. BERRING, HOW TO FIND THE LAW 432 - 512 (8th ed., 1983).
M. JACOBSTEIN & R. MERSKY, FUNDAMENTALS OF LEGAL RESEARCH 100 - 127, 303 - 343 (1987 ed.).
C. KUNZ et al., THE PROCESS OF LEGAL RESEARCH 11 - 48 (1986).

Practice Research Using *A.L.R.*

Use the *A.L.R.* indexes and digests and search the full text of *A.L.R.* annotations on the LEXIS service to find annotations pertinent to the following problems.

1. Your client is the proprietor of a private golf course. A guest of one of the members was injured by a golf ball hit by a caddy. The club does not pay the caddies but has rules that all caddies must obey. One of the rules forbids caddies to hit golf balls. What is the potential liability of the proprietor for the actions of the caddy?

2. Your client discovered that the company doctor called her personal physician to discuss a health problem listed in her employment record. She is upset by the disclosure of information from her employment files, even to her own doctor. She wants to know if she has a right of action against the employer or company doctor.

3. You have just begun private practice in South Carolina. A state court appoints you to represent an indigent person in a civil action. You are to receive no fee. Must you serve without fee?

4. Your client is a 30-year old. He recently contracted an illness that has left him severely disabled and unable to support himself. His parents are refusing to provide any financial support. Are there special circumstances that may revive the parents' duty to support the adult son?

5. For the Billboard Problem, find *A.L.R.* annotations that discuss the application of state law within an Indian reservation.

Using Citators

After you find a case or statute that is pertinent to your research, you must determine if the authority is still "good law." You may be professionally negligent if you base your work for a client on a case that has been reversed or overruled or a statute that is no longer in effect. Has a higher court reversed a decision on appeal? Have later cases limited or expanded the holding of a case? How have courts and administrators interpreted a statute?

Citators help you determine if a case or statute remains good law. Citators also identify additional sources that help you place the case or statute in the context of other primary authority. Citators perform a mechanical function of informing you of the existence of separate but related authority.

This chapter describes three different citator services: Shepard's Citations Service (both in hard copy and online), Auto-Cite and the LEXIS service as a citator.

Using Shepard's Citations Service

Shepard's is the most widely used traditional citator. The red volumes of Shepard's Citations Service are usually shelved by the primary authority that they trace or in a central location in the law library. After you identify a pertinent case, use Shepard's to find the subsequent history of the case and later opinions that cite the case. You also turn to Shepard's to update statutes, administrative regulations, law reviews and patents that have been the subject of litigation.

Shepardizing Cases with the Hardcopy Version

The following steps are necessary to Shepardize cases in the hardcopy service.[1]

---

[1]A note on terminology: The cited case is the case you have found. You wish to find the citing sources, the cases, law review articles, etc., that cite to the case you have found.

STEP 1

First, identify the Shepard's volumes that you will use. Shepard's arranges the cited cases and the coverage of the citing sources by jurisdiction, reporter or area of law. If you wish to see how a California case has been cited, use *Shepard's California Citations* (or, as explained below, *Shepard's Pacific Reporter Citations* or *Shepard's California Reporter Citations*). *Shepard's Federal Labor Law Citations* is an example of a citator arranged by subject.

If you have a federal case citation, choose the Shepard's set that covers the reporter that will be cited. If you begin with a state case, there may be two or more hardcopy reporters that have reported the same case — the reporter for the state, the regional reporter and sometimes a third reporter. Shepard's has a citator for each reporter series, and each provides slightly different coverage of citing sources.

Shepard's coverage for each parallel cite can be different.

It may seem peculiar that the Shepard's citators for the same case vary in content depending on which of the parallel citations you use for the cited case. But there is a purpose for the difference in coverage, as shown in the following example. *People ex rel. Dep't of Transp. v. Naegele Outdoor Advertising Co.*, the case that is the basis of the Billboard Problem, is reported in several printed reporters. Two citations at which the case is reported are 38 Cal.3d 509 (in the official California reporter) and 698 P.2d 150 (in the regional reporter).

If you Shepardize the *Naegele* case in *Shepard's California Citations* using the *Cal.3d* cite, you find citations to the following types of materials:

1. Decisions of California state courts that cite to *Naegele.*
2. Federal courts that cite to *Naegele.*
3. California state attorney general opinions that cite to *Naegele.*
4. Law reviews and legal periodicals published in California and 20 selected law reviews with national reputations that cite to *Naegele.*[2]
5. Any *A.L.R.* annotation that cites to or reports *Naegele.*

If you shepardize the *Naegele* case in the *Shepard's Pacific Reporter Citations* you find citations to the following types of materials:

1. Cases reported in any of the regional reporters, regardless of state, that cite to *Naegele.*
2. Federal cases that cite to *Naegele.*
3. Any *A.L.R.* annotation that cites to or reports *Naegele.*

Although the state citator covers more types of materials, the regional reporter covers citing cases in jurisdictions from a much larger geographic area. You may wish to begin with the state citator to determine the appellate history and how courts within the juris-

---

[2]The coverage for each Shepard's Citator is listed near the beginning of the Shepard's volume. The 20 selected law reviews are listed at page 274 in *Fundamentals of Legal Research* (1987 ed.).

diction have treated the holding of your case. Recall that the appellate history and treatment by other courts within the jurisdiction determine if the holding is still good law within the jurisdiction. The regional citator is just as important, however. The regional citator may provide persuasive authority and broader coverage. More importantly, the regional citator is published on a different schedule and may have more recent cases, even within the jurisdiction, than the state citator. For example, the author and editor of this Manual checked the state and regional citators for the *Naegele* case on the same day. The citator for the regional reporter, *P.2d*, referred to a pending appeal in the federal courts. The state citator, *Cal.3d*, did not mention the appeal.

STEP 2

The second step to using Shepard's Citations Service in the hard copy is to identify the volumes and supplements to use. Choose the volumes by the cites and dates they cover. The cover of each volume and supplement describes what volumes to check. Remember, the supplement you skip might be the one that states your case is overruled!

RESEARCH HINT

Shepard's is not difficult to use. The only real way of learning is to follow the guides in the front and do it!

STEP 3

The third step to using the Shepard's Citations Service in hard copy is to find the actual citator entry for your case. Find the section covering the reporter. Be certain you identify the correct reporter series. Many frustrated researchers swear a case has never been cited and are embarrassed to find that they have been looking at the listing for *38 Cal.2d* instead of *38 Cal.3d*. The cited cases are listed by volume and the page on which the case begins.

8

38C3d509

(213CaR247)
(698P2d154)

US cert den
in106SC1260
s88L Ɛ 453
s106SC520

The entry for each cited case is simply a list of citations with symbols and abbreviations.

Parallel Citations — The first cites listed in parentheses are the parallel citations to the cited case. The parallel citations do not appear in later supplements.

History of the Case — The next citations, if any, give prior or subsequent history of the case. Shepard's editorial abbreviations state if the case has been affirmed, modified, superseded, reversed, vacated or denied certiorari. History letters may also indicate other locations where the same case or a connected case to the cited opinion have been reported. Shepard's also shows special history designations, such as petitions or writs granted, for many jurisdictions. For example, special abbreviations advise California attorneys when review or rehearing has been granted in a case within that state's courts. In the Billboard Problem, both the state and regional Shepard's now state that the *Naegele* case was denied certiorari by the U.S. Supreme Court. They also list several parallel cites to reports of an earlier ruling in the same case.

f216CaR^{3}62
Cir. 9
h625FS^{7}108

List of Citing Cases — Shepard's editors have developed their own system of abbreviations to compact a large amount of information about the citing cases in a small amount of space. The abbreviations appear on the left of the citation and describe how the citing case treated the cited case. For example, "f" means that the citing case followed the original case, applying the *Naegele* holding as controlling law.

Shepard's also helps you identify the exact point of law for which a case is being cited. The editors at Shepard's carefully read the context in which a case is being cited. They then review the headnotes of the cited case to determine which headnote or headnotes best summarize the point of law for which the case is discussed in the citing case, and the appropriate headnote numbers are included in Shepard's. The example includes a "3" shown in superscript to the right of the reporter abbreviation. The "3" tells you that the *Naegele* opinion is cited in conjunction with the third issue of law in the *Naegele* case.

Just reading the Shepard's entry gives you much information about the *Naegele* case. But one of Shepard's primary functions is to inform you of related authority. You should review the text of cases that comprise the history of *Naegele* or that cite *Naegele*. As pointed out in *Fundamentals of Legal Research*,[3] you should read the cases you have found through Shepard's. You must apply or distinguish a case based on a thorough reading of the opinion.

Using the Shepard's Citations Service for Statutes and Other Materials

The Shepard's citators for constitutions, statutes and regulations are organized and used much like the case citators. Choose the appropriate jurisdiction and check the volumes and supplements for amendments or court decisions which have cited the statute. The patent and law review citators also are similar. All you need to begin is the number of the patent or the cite to the law review article.

Use the citators for special subject areas in the same way you use other citators. For example, *Shepard's Corporation Law Citations* provides citations to federal and state corporate law decisions and state statutes that deal with corporations. Citators for subject areas usually include citations from specialized services, law reviews or periodicals in the same area of law as the citator.

---

[3]JACOBSTEIN & MERSKY, FUNDAMENTALS OF LEGAL RESEARCH 275 (1987 ed.).

Updating Your Shepard's Research

By now you should be acutely aware of the need for your legal research to be current. Using Shepard's is a means of bringing your research up to date.

Sometimes you will need to use more than one bound volume and more than one paperback supplement to Shepardize a citation. The cover of each paperback supplement has a box that lists the volumes and supplements your library should contain. Always check the box to be sure you have all the books you need to complete your research.

The cover of each Shepard's supplement has a box listing the volumes and supplements your library should contain.

Using the Online Version of Shepard's Citations Service

During the 1980's, many of Shepard's citators have been added to the LEXIS service[4] and WESTLAW. Shepardizing online could save time and simplify the process by enabling you to Shepardize a case immediately without leaving your chair.

Using Shepard's on the LEXIS service

There is only one step to Shepardize a citation on the LEXIS service.

It is easy to use Shepard's Citations Service on the LEXIS service. LEXIS search logic, using words and connectors to search for occurrences of words, does not apply. There is only one step: transmit the abbreviation *shep*[5] and the citation. To Shepardize the official citation of the *Naegele* case,

TRANSMIT: *shep 38 cal.3d 509*[6]

The LEXIS service displays the citing sources in a format similar to the printed version and uses similar abbreviations.[7]

---

[4]Mainly case citators are available online. The LEXIS service does have the *Shepard's United States Citations for Patents.* Use the hardcopy Shepard's, annotated codes and LEXIS as citators for statutes. See page 105 for a description of using the LEXIS service as a citator of statutes.

[5]You may substitute the shorter *sh* for *shep*.

[6]If you are uncertain of the citation format, press the h (for help) key after transmitting shep or check the list of Shepard's abbreviations in the *LEXIS/NEXIS Reference Manual.*

[7]Some cases are so frequently cited that the Shepard's list continues over many LEXIS screens. If you wish to limit the Shepard's display to the history of the cited case and those citing sources for which the editors have assigned treatment codes (such as "distinguished," "followed" or "overruled"), press the SEGMTS (for segments) key and TRANSMIT: *any*

Shepardize the parallel citations.

Although you do not choose a citator or sort through the hard-copy volumes and supplements when you use Shepard's on the LEXIS service, you still must Shepardize the parallel citations separately to assure thorough and current coverage. For example, after Shepardizing the official cite to *Naegele, 38 Cal.3d 509,* you should also Shepardize the parallel cite for the regional reporter, *698 P.2d 150.* The reasons for Shepardizing both the official and regional citations if you are using Shepard's on the LEXIS service are the same as if you are using the printed version: the coverage of citing sources is different and one citator may be more current. In the *Naegele* example, Shepardizing the official cite gives you a citation to a law review article the regional citator does not cover.

RESEARCH HINT

To Shepardize a case you are viewing on the LEXIS service, just

TRANSMIT: *shep*

It is not necessary to enter the cite. Then, when you are ready to return from Shepard's to the case you were viewing,

TRANSMIT: *resume lexis*

Get into the habit of Shepardizing a case as soon as you believe it is pertinent to your research. In general, you save time if you read the most recent cases early in your research because the most recent cases often cite and discuss the earlier law.

Viewing Citing Cases on the LEXIS Service

You should read the cases you have found through Shepard's. Each citing case listed on the Shepard's display on the LEXIS service is numbered. To view the text of a citing case, simply transmit the appropriate number from the column on the far left of the screen. For example, below is the Shepard's entry for one of the cases citing the *Naegele* case.

NUMBER	ANALYSIS	CITING REFERENCE
8	harmonized	625 F. Supp. 108.

To immediately see the portion of this case that cites to the *Naegele* case,

TRANSMIT: *8*

When you are ready to return to the Shepard's list,

TRANSMIT: *resume shep*

Auto-Cite on the LEXIS Service

Auto-Cite fulfills a number of research functions. Like using other citators, you begin with a cite. Auto-Cite gives you information about the case that is different from the information other citators give you. You may use Auto-Cite to verify that a citation is accurate (are the spelling of the parties' names, the court and the year of decision correct?), to confirm that the holdings of the case are still good law (was there an appeal or did a holding of a later case affect the validity of the holding?) or as a research aid (does an *A.L.R.* annotation discuss the issue?).

Auto-Cite covers American cases from 1658 to date.

Auto-Cite is an online service. There is no printed version, although the commercial service evolved from a manual cite-checking system created and used for decades by the editorial staff of Lawyers Co-operative Publishing Company.[8] Auto-Cite covers American cases from 1658 to date, more than 300 reporters. You may begin with a LEXIS Cite or a cite to an official, unofficial or topical reporter. Then Auto-Cite responds with the following:

- The case name, jurisdiction and year of decision
- Parallel citations
- The prior and subsequent history of the case, e.g., lower courts, appellate courts and decisions on remand
- References to related proceedings involving the same parties
- Citations of cases that directly affect the validity of the holding of the case
- Citations of prior cases to which the case you entered makes a negative reference
- Citations to pertinent *A.L.R.* and *L.Ed.* annotations

Auto-Cite does not attempt to list all the cases that cite your case. But Auto-Cite may list a *Case A* that does not cite your case if a later *Case B* describes the impact of the holding of *Case A* on the validity of the holding in your case.[9]

RESEARCH HINT

Even with word-processing, it is easy for the names of the parties, the court or date of decision to be incorrect in the final draft of a brief, memorandum or article. Many law firms, courts and agencies require that every case cited in a final document be verified in Auto-Cite. Develop the habit of checking all the citations in the final draft of your law school work on Auto-Cite.

---

[8]A similar online service, called Insta-Cite, has been developed to accompany the WESTLAW service.

[9]A court might overrule or narrow the holding of an earlier case without explicitly criticizing or even citing the prior case.

Using Auto-Cite with the LEXIS Service

Like the online version of Shepard's, Auto-Cite is easy to use. You begin with a cite. At any point in your LEXIS research you can transmit *ac* and the cite you wish to verify. For example, to use Auto-Cite for the *Naegele* case, simply

TRANSMIT: *ac 38 cal.3d 509*

You may enter any of the parallel citations and retrieve the same results. LEXIS search logic -- using words and connectors to search for occurrences of words -- does not apply.

```
Auto-Cite Service, Copyright (c) 1988, VERALEX INC.:
38 CAL3D 509:

People ex rel. Dept. of Transportation v Naegele Outdoor Advertising Co. (1985)
38 Cal 3d 509, 213 Cal Rptr 247, 698 P2d 150, cert den California Dept. of
Transp. v Naegele Outdoor Advertising Co. (1986) 475 US 1045, 89 L Ed 2d 570,
106 S Ct 1260, 54 USLW 3582

PRIOR HISTORY:
People ex rel. Dept. of Transportation v Naegele Outdoor Advertising Co. (1984,
4th Dist) 152 Cal App 3d 516, 199 Cal Rptr 605, superseded, en banc (BY
CITATION YOU ENTERED)
```

The entry in Auto-Cite for the *Naegele* case.

If you enter the citation of an *A.L.R.* annotation instead of the cite to a case, the Auto-Cite response tells you if the annotation has been superseded, partially superseded or supplemented by a more recent annotation and refers you to annotations on related topics.

> **TIME-SAVING TIP**
>
> To see the Auto-Cite entry for a case you are viewing on the LEXIS service, just
>
> TRANSMIT: *ac*
>
> It is not necessary to enter the cite. Get into the habit of using both Auto-Cite and Shepard's when you first believe a case is pertinent to your research.

Viewing Cases and Annotations You Find through Auto-Cite

An Auto-Cite entry may refer you to cases, statutes and *A.L.R.* or *L.Ed.* annotations. As with any other citator, you must judge the relevance of authority to your issue by reading the authority. The editors of a citator service do not know your issue or how you plan to use a given case when they describe its treatment. To view the cases or annotations referred to in an Auto-Cite entry, use the LEXSEE feature. To view a statute, use the LEXSTAT feature. For example, the Auto-Cite entry for the *Naegele* case refers to *152 Cal. App. 3d 516.* To see the report of this case,

TRANSMIT: *lexsee 152 cal. app. 3d 516*

Read the authorities to determine their relevance to your issue.

Using Auto-Cite and Shepard's Citations Service

Auto-Cite and the online version of Shepard's provide different information in response to the entry of a citation. Some of the information, such as parallel citations, is duplicative but most of the information is unique to each service. Both services assist you in linking related authorities and in understanding your case in the context of other authorities. Because the features and depth and breadth of coverage are so different, no simple comparison is adequate. Although Shepard's has been available in print since 1873, and Auto-Cite is based upon a manual system which has been in use for nearly a century, the online versions of both services are relatively new and practicing attorneys are still determining how these services fit into their research needs. You can determine for yourself. At different points in your research, print the Auto-Cite and Shepard's entries for materials that you find. Determine if they save you time and find relevant authority.

LEXIS as a Citator

The LEXIS service can find cited materials and citing materials not covered by other citators.

To use Shepard's and Auto-Cite you enter a cite and receive a prepared response. You use the LEXIS service as a citator by searching the full text of a file for occurrences of a citation. You can search for a cite to virtually any source in files of legal and non-legal information.

There are several reasons to use the LEXIS service as a citator. Your research is more thorough when the LEXIS service is used in conjunction with the other citators. You also can find cited materials (such as case references to medical textbooks or census statistics) and citing materials (such as some unpublished court and administrative decisions or newspaper articles) that are not covered by other citators.

Using the LEXIS Service to Find Citations to Cases

Cases may be cited in a variety of sources: other cases, administrative decisions and rulings, U.S. Supreme Court briefs, law reviews, newspapers and newsletters. The LEXIS service sometimes can fill gaps in citing materials that other citators do not cover.

The LEXIS service may find references to a case in very recent or unpublished cases and administrative rulings. The technique is

Search for occurrences of a unique word pattern in the cite —

~~People ex rel Dep't of~~ Transp. ~~v.~~ Naegele ~~Outdoor Advertising Co.~~

the same used to develop any LEXIS search. Envision how a case or other legal document may cite to the case. Then develop a search for the unique word pattern in that cite. For example, a search for references to the *Naegele* case could be, e.g.,

TRANSMIT: transp OR *transportation* W/10 *naegele*

The case that is the basis of the Tax Problem is *United States v. 1954 Rolls Royce,* 777 F.2d 1358 (9th Cir. 1985). A search for references to either the name of the case or the citation could be, e.g.,

TRANSMIT: *1954 rolls royce* OR *(777* PRE/5 *1358*)

The above search is for the phrase "1954 rolls royce" or, as an alternative, an occurrence of the word "777" five or less searchable words before "1358." Note the difference between the standard citation form and the sample search request. Many terms in the citation have been left out of the search. Such a search may find cases that do not cite to *777 F.2d 1358*. But it is better to err on the side of *inclusion* (retrieving more cases) than *exclusion* (missing a relevant case that may vary from standard citation form). Use the KWIC display to browse through the retrieved cases to determine if they cite to your case. If you find too many irrelevant occurrences of the search terms, you can modify by adding terms pertinent to the issue. In the above example, the modification could be, e.g.,

It is better to err on the side of *inclusion* than *exclusion.*

TRANSMIT: *m*
TRANSMIT: W/50 *seiz!* OR *forfeit!*

RESEARCH HINT

Keep a record of the cases you find using the LEXIS service as a citator to compare to the list of cases you find by other means. Your records should include the date of the search and the names of the LEXIS libraries and files that you search.

Search all the files of primary and secondary authorities that may cite to your case. Both federal and state court cases cite to the California state court decision in the *Naegele* case, so you must search both federal and state LEXIS files for references to *Naegele.*

Sometimes a case is cited frequently, e.g., the landmark case of *Miranda v. Arizona,* and you want to determine if a case has applied the holding to a specific fact situation. The LEXIS service is an ideal complement to traditional citators for such problems. You can use the LEXIS service to search through the thousands of cases that cite *Miranda*[10] to determine if any have applied the require-

[10]Some cases may refer to a landmark case, such as *Miranda* or *Erie*, in a non-standard format. For example, an opinion may refer to the "*Miranda* ruling" or "*Miranda* warning" and never actually cite the case. A carefully formulated LEXIS search can find such non-standard references.

ments of *Miranda* to arrests made in mobile homes. A possible search is, e.g.,

TRANSMIT: *miranda* W/50 *mobile* W/3 *home*

You can combine the use of the LEXIS service as a citator with any other LEXIS search. For example, you can find how a particular judge or court has treated an important case by searching for opinions written by the judge that also cite the case.

The LEXIS and NEXIS services also can find references to cases in non-legal materials. For example, many politicians, judges and lawyers have been quoted or have written newspaper articles and letters to the editor regarding the landmark case of *Miranda v. Arizona*. You can find these articles in *The New York Times* by searching the NEXIS file for references to the *Miranda* decision. Just remember that, although the *The New York Times* gives the case name and docket number in reports of recent U.S. Supreme Court cases, most newspaper articles about the *Miranda* decision will not use the citation format of a law review or case. Simply devise a search for variations of the words and word patterns you think will occur in the article.

Using the LEXIS Service to Find Citations to Statutes and Regulations

You use the LEXIS service as a citator to statutes and regulations[11] for the same reasons you use LEXIS to complement case citators. Searching for references to statutes requires attention to how a court might refer to the statute. Will the opinion refer to the name of the act, the *Statutes at Large*, or the title and section of the code? If the court cites to a title and section of the federal code, will it be the official version (U.S.C.), or one of the two annotated commercial versions (U.S.C.S. or U.S.C.A.)? Begin with the reference you think is most likely to appear in a case, ruling or article that applies or discusses the statute.

For example, in the Tax Problem the court is likely to refer to Section 7302 of the Internal Revenue Code. The cases in which you are interested will likely be in the LEXIS Federal Tax library. You might search, e.g.,

TRANSMIT: *7302* OR §*7302*[12]

Cases that cite to titles of the U.S. Code other than the tax code usually include the title number. For example, one section of the

---

[11]See Chapter Six for a description of using the LEXIS service to find authorities citing regulations.

[12]Why this configuration? Courts might refer to the statutory section with or without a space between the section symbol and the number. Remember that spacing is important in full-text searching. A search for *7302* retrieves occurrences of *§ 7302* or *Section 7302* but does not find occurrences of a cite to the section without a space after the section symbol, *§7302*.

8

codified *Highway Beautification Act* is *23 U.S.C. § 319.* A court could cite to this section in a number of ways:

23 U.S.C. § 319
23 U.S. Code § 319
23 U.S.C.S. § 319
23 U.S.C.A. § 319
Sections 131 and 319 of Title 23

One search that finds the above variations in citation form is, e.g.,

TRANSMIT: *23* W/10 *319* OR §*319*

The technique of adding relevant terms to augment LEXIS searches for case citations also applies to searches for citations to a statute. For example, you may wish to find any reference to the word "pre-emption" in a case citing 23 U.S.C. § 319. Modify the above search for references to the statute by transmitting *m* and, e.g.,

TRANSMIT: AND *preempt!* OR *pre empt!*

Using the LEXIS Service to Find Citations to Rules, Constitutions and Other Sources

The ability of the LEXIS service to search for virtually any word or word pattern enables you to find citations to any source in primary or secondary authority.

The federal and many state constitutions use both Roman numerals and Arabic numbers in their numbering schemes. Neither cardinal and ordinal numbers, nor Roman numerals and Arabic numbers, are treated as equivalents by the LEXIS service. Therefore, a search for citations to the Fourteenth Amendment to the U.S. Constitution might include, e.g.,

TRANSMIT: *amendment* W/5 *14* OR *14th* OR *xiv* OR *xivth*

Often a litigator wants to find instances in which a federal rule was applied in a certain situation. The LEXIS service can be very useful in citing to federal rules in different contexts. Because courts routinely refer to rules, the format of citations to the Federal Rules of Civil Procedure varies widely. One search that finds most references to, e.g., Rule 23, is

TRANSMIT: *rule* OR *civ* OR *frcp* OR *f.r.c.p.* W/5 *23*

RESEARCH HINTS

Look at citation formats as you read cases and articles. Note the differences and develop your LEXIS search to find the variant forms of citation.

Remember to search files of administrative law, law review articles and the *A.L.R.* and *L.Ed.* annotations when you use the LEXIS service as a citator.

Often you want to know if a court has ever used or interpreted information or sources that you find in your research. For example, you may wish to know if a court has ever relied on the work of an economist in deciding an anti-trust case. Many of the authorities discussed in this book, including legislative histories, Presidential Executive Orders, treaties, and the American Bar Association's *Model Rules of Professional Conduct* are cited by courts and other authorities. Some of the traditional citators can assist you in finding citations to these disparate sources.[13] Searching the full text of authorities for citations can supplement the coverage of the traditional citators and, in some instances, be the only means to find citations to the source.

Using LEXIS as a citator can complement traditional citators and sometimes be the only means to find citations.

The accompanying list has just a few of the sources that you can find cited in authorities with the LEXIS service. Again, use the approach to searching the full text that is described in this Manual. Envision the different ways the source may be cited and formulate a search that finds the words or word patterns that are embodied in the various forms of the citation.

LEXIS can be used to find cites to the following sources in legal authorities:

legislative histories
treaties and conventions
International Court of Justice
Ethical Considerations (E.C.'s)
Presidential Executive Orders
Financial Accounting Standards Board — statements and interpretations
local court rules
textbooks
medical texts
experts and professors

Diagnostic & Statistical Manual (DSM-III)
administrative decisions and rulings
local ordinances
Uniform Commercial Code
restatements of the law
treatises
state statutes
hornbooks

[13]For example, the *ABA/BNA Manual on Professional Conduct* and *Shepard's Professional and Judicial Conduct Citations* can assist you in finding citations to ethical rules and formal and informal opinions of the Committee on Legal Ethics of the Amercian Bar Association.

Summary

You must check each authority on which you rely to ensure that it remains good law and that you have identified all pertinent resources. You must learn how to use Shepard's (both the hard copy and online version), Auto-Cite and the LEXIS service as a citator. They complement each other in finding related authority, placing authority in the context of other authority and providing a measure of completeness in your research.

The best means of understanding citators is to use them. If you have not yet used citators, you may wish to reread this chapter or the related readings after you have gained some experience.

RELATED READINGS

M. JACOBSTEIN & R. MERSKY, FUNDAMENTALS OF LEGAL RESEARCH 269 - 302 (1987 ed.).
M. COHEN & R. BERRING, HOW TO FIND THE LAW 249 - 285 (8th ed., 1983).
C. KUNZ et al., THE PROCESS OF LEGAL RESEARCH 74 - 86, 118 - 122 (1986).

Practice Research in Using Citators

1. Check *People ex rel. Dep't of Transp. v. Naegele Outdoor Advertising Co.*, 38 Cal. 3d 509, to see if it is still good law by using:
   - Shepard's Citations Service
     - Manually
     - Online
   - Auto-Cite
   - The LEXIS Service as a Citator

2. On a psychiatric issue, your expert refers to the *Statistical and Diagnostic Manual.* He explains that psychiatric illnesses are categorized and defined in this generally-accepted manual. You want to know if courts rely on the definitions and classification scheme of the *Diagnostic and Statistical Manual.* Use traditional tools and the LEXIS service to find judicial references to the *Manual.*

Specialized Legal Research

Critics of the legal profession lament the demise of the solo practitioner who considered his clients to be personal friends and counseled them in all legal matters from birth to death. The growing complexity of society and our laws make it difficult for a solo attorney to be a competent counsel for a client's wide spectrum of legal matters. This growth has resulted in attorneys who specialize in a specific area or type of law.

Lawyers are also recognizing the danger of practicing law in highly technical, unfamiliar areas. The *Model Code of Professional Responsibility* specifically forbids attorneys from handling legal issues they are not competent to handle.[1] When attorneys encounter a situation they believe they lack the expertise to handle, they should refer the client to a lawyer who has a stronger background in that area of law.

Rather than refer away lucrative business, many firms are growing by adding attorneys with expertise in as many specialized areas of practice as are required to provide full legal services to their clients.

Although you may have entered law school knowing you want to practice in a particular field, most students are "generalists" and sample a variety of legal subject areas during law school. No matter what your current plans are, someday you may need to acquire expertise in a special area of law.

Thus it is important that you understand the basics of specialized legal research. This chapter outlines these concepts and presents several special subject areas as examples of the materials and resources available in these specialized fields.

---

[1]*See* MODEL CODE OF PROFESSIONAL RESPONSIBILITY Canon 6.

Specialization and Legal Research

In most ways, legal research in specialized fields is no different than other legal research. You interpret authorities with which you are familiar, such as court decisions and statutes.

However, specialization creates unique information requirements, sources and research tools. These special materials can appear to be a complex and intimidating mystery to the neophyte researcher, but are basic resources that some lawyers use almost daily.

From the beginning, practitioners realized that a solution to specialization was to collect, in a single place, cases and documents relevant to a particular area of law. Sometimes publishers identified the pertinent materials, arranged the materials, and sold them as specialized volumes. This resulted in the same case being found in two places, a generalized reporter as well as a specialized volume. The same approach has been used in the creation of online systems.

Typically, specialized research tools gather together pertinent information an attorney needs to practice in a particular area. By narrowing the focus of the search, the attorney eliminates clutter, saves research time, and keeps current with the wide range of activities within the specialty.

For example, tax attorneys concentrate their research on tax laws, tax regulations, court decisions on tax issues, I.R.S. revenue rulings, and other I.R.S. documentation. In researching a tax issue, does it make more sense to search for tax cases in a general database or reporter system, or to concentrate on specialized databases and reporters that include only tax materials? The answer in most instances is to zero in on the tax materials.

Keep in mind that part of becoming a specialist will be learning the "tools of the trade." You will concentrate on the special, pertinent authorities that govern an area of law. For example, a securities lawyer has a solid background in the Securities Act of 1933 and the Securities Exchange Act of 1934. Some lawyers might specialize further, becoming experts in a particular area of securities such as municipal bonds.

Looseleaf Services

The one research tool that is common to almost every field of legal specialization is the looseleaf. Chapter Six mentions looseleafs in connection with administrative law research. An attorney specializing in a particular area soon learns to depend on looseleaf services that cover his or her area.

Looseleaf publications combine available sources of law on a specific subject matter. For example, in the *BNA Pension Reporter*,[2]

---

[2]The *BNA Pension Reporter* is a weekly notification service that covers the latest pension developments nationwide.

lawyers find the statutes, regulations, and case law pertinent to pension law.

Looseleaf services provide a thorough collection of authorities in a subject area, so it is not necessary to search through the entire *United States Code* or the *Code of Federal Regulations.*[3] Since several publishers provide tax looseleafs of primary authorities in tax, attorneys usually choose the one they feel provides the best editorial comment and research aids.

Looseleafs also keep the attorney abreast of new developments in the law. A looseleaf routinely provides the attorney with releases, which are pages supplementing the original looseleaf. The release gives a thorough review of the latest activity in the legal subjects covered by the specialized looseleaf. Specialists keep informed in their area by reading the new pages provided by each supplement.

There are a few difficulties in using looseleafs. The filing of new pages can be a time-consuming process and a careless filer may mix or discard pages in error.

RESEARCH HINT

If you approach a looseleaf set as a novice, you should take some time to read the instructions. Each looseleaf has unique features and arrangements that can confuse the first-time user. Determining a basic fact such as whether the index refers you to a page or paragraph number can save you valuable time and limit your frustration.

Specialized Databases

The LEXIS service has created specialized online libraries to help you focus your legal research on certain areas of law. Like the subject looseleafs, these special libraries bring together court decisions, statutes, administrative decisions, regulations and other pertinent documents on specific areas of law. By narrowing the scope of the documents you are searching and bringing to one library a complete set of relevant materials, the specialized libraries help you perform more accurate and more complete searches.

The specialized libraries are often more complete in their coverage, going back in time and including materials not in the general libraries. Some of the specialized libraries include secondary authority — editorial summaries and commentary — provided by private publishers such as The Bureau of National Affairs, Inc.

[3]For a selected listing of looseleaf reporting services *see* M. JACOBSTEIN & R. MERSKY, FUNDAMENTALS OF RESEARCH Appendix F 688-697 (1987 ed.) or R. Berring & V. Weden, *Looseleaf Services: A Subject Bibliography*, 1 L. REF. SERV. Q. 51 (1981).

Specialized libraries also allow the attorney to focus on applicable authority quickly, reducing the retrieval of extraneous information. Searching in the Environmental Law library for an issue from the Billboard Problem may simplify the retrieval of information dealing with environmental issues. This eliminates the need to use forms of "environment" as a search concept, since the cases in the Environmental Law library have been selected to limit irrelevant cases.

For example, suppose you are representing a hospital in California. The hospital administrators ask you what the California law is concerning the discontinuance of life support to terminally ill patients. You could use the Health Law library in the LEXIS service to do the following search.

LIBRARY: HEALTH

FILE: CAL (includes California health care cases)

TRANSMIT: *life support* W/10 *discontinu!* OR *dis continu!* OR *terminat!* OR *end!* OR *plug!* OR *unplug!*

You do not have to add words to give the search a medical framework. By searching in the Health Law library you have directed your search to documents dealing with health care.

A Brief Description of Several Specialized Subject Areas

Tax Law

Tax is one of the most popular specialized areas of practice. The complex regulations, ever-changing laws, specialized courts and significant sums involved in tax law discourage the generalist and create a need for lawyers who are thoroughly familiar with tax law. Tax lawyers are heavily dependent upon the specialized tools of looseleafs and specialized databases.

The Code Approach to Tax Research

Attorneys and accountants often are extremely familiar with the Internal Revenue Code and regulations by their section number. These specialists immediately recognize the sections pertinent to specific tax issues, and cite the sections with a familiarity that confounds the uninitiated. For example, a tax attorney faced with the Tax Problem would immediately think of Section 7302 of the Internal Revenue Code (Title 26 of the *U.S.C.)*.

This automatic referral to sections of the Code allows much of tax literature to be arranged by Code section numbers. Popular looseleafs like the Commerce Clearing House, Inc.'s *Standard Fed-*

eral Tax Reporter[4] and Prentice-Hall, Inc.'s *Federal Taxes*[5] arrange their information under sections of the Code. This allows the tax researcher to turn directly to the part of the looseleaf that pertains to a section to read the applicable text of the Code, editorial comments, pertinent cases, and revenue rulings for a thorough understanding of the law in that particular area. The general practitioner, who does not have a tax specialist's familiarity with the Code, might use The Research Institute of America, Inc.'s *Federal Tax Coordinator 2d.*[6] That set is arranged by subject rather than by code section. This is particularly helpful where tax concepts transcend any single code section.

The code approach can also be used in online searching. The tax attorney interested in Section 7302 could easily search one of the case law files in the FEDTAX library of the LEXIS service for:

active W/3 *aid* AND *7302* OR §*7302*

Courts, general commentators, and Internal Revenue Service documents use "7302" as a buzz word to indicate the concept embodied in that particular section of the code. The above search would retrieve documents discussing that section which may never mention it by its formal heading: "Property Used in Violation of Internal Revenue Laws."

Tax Courts

Tax research is also unusual in its overlay of court systems. In most instances, you can elect to present a tax case before a United States District Court, the United States Claims Court, or the United States Tax Court.

There are several basic factors that determine which court to choose. Your client can present a case in the Tax Court without prepaying the disputed amount, while the District Court and the Claims Court require you to pay the amount before you sue for a refund. Tax Court judges specialize in taxation and their decisions are generally considered to be more valuable as precedent than the decisions of the other two courts.

Appeals from the U.S. District Courts and the Tax Court are taken to the United States Court of Appeals. Cases appealed from the Claims Court are heard by the United States Court of Appeals for the Federal Circuit.

Court decisions are reported in the looseleafs noted above, in specialized reporters such as *CCH U.S. Tax Cases, Federal Tax Reports*, and online in the Federal Tax (FEDTAX) library of the LEXIS service.

9

---

[4]CCH STANDARD FEDERAL TAX REPORTER (Commerce Clearing House, Inc. 1989).

[5]P-H FEDERAL TAXES (Prentice-Hall, 1988).

[6]FEDERAL TAX COORDINATOR, 2d ed., (Research Institute of America, 1987).

- Basic treatises in the tax law:

J. Chommie, *Federal Income Taxation* (2d ed. 1973).
C. Lowndes, R. Kramer, & J. McCord, *Federal Estate & Gift Taxes* (1974).
J. Mertens & R. E. Paul, *The Law of Federal Income Taxation* (1942-).
D. Posin, *Federal Income Taxation of Individuals and Basic Concepts in the Taxation of All Entities* (1983).
J. Rabkin & M. Johnson, *Federal Income, Gift & Estate Taxation* (1987).

- Basic databases in tax law:

Many of the original efforts to create full-text legal databases began in the area of tax. The dependency of the tax accountant and attorney on specific sections of the code, the highly specialized language, and the inadequacy of government-generated indexes made tax law a natural candidate for full-text searching.

The first online tax database was the FEDTAX library on the LEXIS service. Today it includes more than 75 files, including Title 26 of the U.S. Code, proposed and final tax regulations, tax cases from all federal and state courts, legislative documents for tax legislation, tax treaties, revenue rulings, looseleaf services and newsletters.

Another tax database is PHINET, which includes Prentice-Hall's tax materials and publications.

- Basic research in tax law:

Your first tax course will introduce you to a new world of documents which are intrinsic to tax research. The following is a partial list of these materials.

Rulings

When the Internal Revenue Service is presented with a specific fact situation, it issues rulings which answer the question posed by the problem. When the rulings are directed to the general public they are called revenue rulings. Rulings directed to individual taxpayers are known as private letter rulings.

Although revenue rulings do not officially bind the Internal Revenue Service in future decisions, they are generally followed as an indication of how the Service will interpret the tax law in similar situations. Private letter rulings cannot be generalized. Until 1977, private letter rulings were unavailable to the general public. Since that time they have been available in many of the looseleaf services as well as in the LEXIS FEDTAX library.

Internal Revenue Bulletin; Cumulative Bulletin

This is the official service published by the Internal Revenue Service. Perhaps more than any other title it is the tax lawyer's official guidebook. Published weekly, it contains revenue rulings, proposed and finalized regulations, pertinent Supreme Court decisions, legislative history for tax legislation, tax treaties, and various other documents necessary to keep aware of Internal Revenue Service actions. The weekly issues are replaced by the *Cumulative Bulletin* every six months.

Looseleafs and Newsletters

Tax looseleafs provide comprehensive coverage of the code, regulations, cases, and developing areas of tax law. The most popular titles in the field are the *CCH Standard Federal Tax Reporter* and Prentice-Hall's *Federal Taxes*. The BNA *Tax Management Portfolios* are highly regarded commentaries on particular tax topics.

The need for tax practitioners to be informed of the latest developments has made tax newsletters an additional special research tool. Unlike the traditional tax looseleafs, newsletters do not seek to be complete tax libraries, but serve as a current awareness tool for the tax specialist. Publishers often provide newsletters as an additional tool to supplement their looseleafs, referring the attorney back to the pertinent section of the standard looseleaf service for complete background on a current development. Online newsletters such as BNA's *Daily Tax Report* and *BNA Tax Update,* Commerce Clearing House, Inc.'s *CCH TAX DAY* and Tax Analysts, Inc.'s *Tax Notes Today* provide tax attorneys daily news and analysis of developments in the area.

■ Related information on tax law and research can be found in:

L. Chanin and P. McDermott, "Federal Income Taxation," in *Specialized Legal Research* (1987).

G. L. Richmond, "Federal Tax Research," in *Fundamentals of Legal Research,* (1987 ed.); expanded in G. L. Richmond, *Federal Tax Research: Guide to Materials and Techniques* (3d ed. 1987).

T. Thomas, *Computer-assisted Legal and Tax Research: A Professional's Guide to LEXIS, WESTLAW, and PHINET* (1986).

Law and Medicine

As a law student, your closest association with medicine may be your annual checkup, but as an attorney your work may often touch on medical issues. Popular stereotypes depict the two professions pitted against each other in malpractice suits. However, many of the leading social and ethical issues of our day involve medical and legal problems which must be studied and solved jointly.

You already may have seen this interplay of disciplines in your law school coursework. In criminal law you might consider the impact of incompetency or criminal insanity; in your contracts course you might ponder the rights and obligations of a surrogate mother; and your constitutional law class might discuss cases dealing with life support systems, abortions, and the right to medical treatment.

Another development in this area is that more students are coming to law school from medical backgrounds. They will use their dual expertise to guide both professions in addressing these developing issues.

Although traditional medical research evolves around complex clinical experiments, the medical field and its publishers produce considerable literature of interest to lawyers. There is also a large body of medical information written for a legal audience in recognition of the lawyer's need to understand medical terms, procedures and issues.

- Basic treatises and tools in law and medicine:

An attorney researching medical issues needs a medical dictionary and explanatory guides like W. Dornette, *Stedman's Medical Dictionary* (5th abr. lawyers ed. 1982) and R. Sloane's, *The Sloane-Dorland Medical-Legal Dictionary* (1987). Faber's Medical Dictionary (15th ed.) has been reprinted as the Am. Jur. *Proof of Facts Medical Dictionary.* A newly-published work is Ausman and Snyder's multi-volume *Medical Library, Lawyer's Edition* (a medical encyclopedia). Well known and respected texts like Gray's *Anatomy of the Human Body* (30th ed. 1984) are references for basic information and background.

There are a variety of legal medicine books available, describing medical procedures and diseases in detail yet in terms comprehensible to the average attorney. Among the most popular is R. Gray, *Attorneys' Textbook of Medicine* (3rd ed. 1987).

Professional journals, perhaps the cornerstones of current medical research, are essential resources. Among the most basic are *JAMA: The Journal of the American Medical Association* and *The New England Journal of Medicine.* Unlike the legal profession, in which the most prestigious journals are published by law schools, many medical journals are published under the auspices of professional medical associations like the Massachusetts Medical Society.

- Basic databases in law and medicine:

Medical research materials are unfamiliar to most lawyers and can be as intimidating as legal materials are to the nonlawyer. The LEXIS service provides a special library and a special medical service, called MEDIS, to help the attorney handle medical information.

The materials available in the MEDIS libraries include medical textbooks and specialized journals. MEDIS also gives you access to MEDLINE, the database of the National Library of Medicine, which provides abstracts from a large variety of medical journals.

The content of the Health Law library in the LEXIS service was defined in conjunction with the American Academy of Hospital Attorneys of the American Hospital Association. It is a full-text, online source for research in health care case law. The Health Law library gives you a comprehensive collection of state and federal case law dealing with various aspects of health care and publications dealing with health law and hospital administration.

Intellectual Property Law

Another highly specialized area of law is intellectual property. It is the body of law that deals with the protection of patents, trademarks, copyright and some aspects of competition.

Most patent lawyers have scientific or technical backgrounds to help them interpret complex patent material. In fact, an attorney must be registered with the Patent and Trademark Office before presenting patent applications to the Office.[7] Any attorney may practice trademark and non-patent law with the Patent and Trademark Office.[8]

■ Basic resources in intellectual property law:

D. S. Chisum, *Patents* (1978).

M. A. Epstein, *Modern Intellectual Property* (1984).

L. Horwitz, *Patent Office Rules & Practice* (1987).

E. B. Lipscomb, *Walker on Patents* (3d ed., 1984).

A. Miller & M. Davis, *Intellectual Property: Patents, Trademarks & Copyright in a Nutshell* (1983).

M.B. Nimmer, *Copyright* (1985).

Department of Commerce, *Manual of Patent Examining Procedure* (5th ed. 3rd rev., 1986) and *Trademark Manual of Examining Procedure* (rev. ed., 1986).

■ Basic databases in intellectual property law:

The LEXPAT library in the LEXIS service provides the full text of U.S. patents and other reference materials. Almost 1500 patents are added to LEXPAT every week, and patents are usually online within six days of issue.

The Patent, Trademark and Copyright Law library in the LEXIS service includes intellectual property cases and administrative opinions from the Patent Administrative Appeal Board. The UKIP file in the United Kingdom library provides English case law on intellectual property.

DIALOG has specialized databases which include abstracts of and information for trademarks and patents. The highly technical patent and trademark areas are supported by several companies which have created their own proprietary databases. Attorneys can

---

[7]To register, an attorney must either pass an examination or serve for four years in the patent examining corps of the Patent and Trademark Office. 37 C.F.R. §10.7.

[8]37 C.F.R. §10.14.

hire these companies to perform database searches for them.[9]

Almost every area of specialty has journals and law reviews dedicated to reporting developments in the field. Among the most important for patent and intellectual property law is the *AIPLA Quarterly Journal*, the *Journal of the American Intellectual Property Law Association*, and the *Intellectual Property Law Review*.[10]

■ Additional reading on copyright research:

J. Beard, "Copyright Law" in *Specialized Legal Research* (1987).

Securities and Corporation Law

Stock market fluctuations heighten our awareness of the complexity of state, national, and international securities markets. An attorney frequently faces clients who ask how to structure business entities to meet their objectives.

Securities law is a very technical area where specialists can concentrate their careers on several sections of the U.S Code.

■ Basic treatises and tools in securities and corporation law:

A. Bromber & L. Lowenfels, *Securities Fraud & Commodities Fraud* (1986).

L. Loss, *Securities Regulation* (2d ed., 1961 - 1969).

L. Loss, *Fundamentals of Securities Regulation* (2d ed.,1988).

D. L. Ratner, *Securities Regulation in a Nutshell* (1982).

■ Basic databases in securities and corporation law:

The LEXIS service provides the Federal Securities Law library which enables full-text searching of the pertinent documentation. The library includes relevant court decisions, federal statutes, and the regulations, decisions, orders, releases, and "no-action" letters of the Securities and Exchange Commission.

Many attorneys find the NAARS service helpful in locating annual reports of firms. It is available through the LEXIS service. Security specialists rely heavily on looseleaf services like the *CCH Federal Securities Law Reporter* and the *Prentice-Hall Securities Regulation Service*.

The *SEC Docket* and the *SEC News Digest* are informative updating services. Originally published by the government, they are

---

[9]Thomson & Thomson in Boston is perhaps the most widely known of this type of proprietary database company. Many of the Thomson databases are available on the DIALOG service.

[10]Other journals include: BNA's PATENT, TRADEMARK & COPYRIGHT JOURNAL, THE COPYRIGHT LAW JOURNAL, JOURNAL OF THE COPYRIGHT SOCIETY OF THE USA, JOURNAL OF THE PATENT AND TRADEMARK OFFICE SOCIETY, and UNITED STATES PATENT QUARTERLY.

currently available through commercial publishers.

At the state level, securities are governed by what are known as "blue sky" laws. The *CCH Blue Sky Law Reporter* gathers the important and sometimes elusive state materials into a single looseleaf title.

There are numerous periodicals on securities law. Among the most popular are *Securities Regulation Law Journal* and *Securities Law Review.*

Additional readings in securities research:

M. A. Sargent & E. R. Greenberg, "Research in Securities Regulation: Access to the Sources of the Law," *75 L. Libr. J. 98* (1982), updated by M.A. Sargent & M. G. Senter, "Research in Securities Regulation Revisited," *79 L. Libr. J. 255* (1987).

McFadden, "Bibliographic Overview of Securities Materials," *1 Legal Ref. Serv. Q. 11* (1981).

K. Todd, "Securities Regulation," in *Specialized Legal Research* (1987).

Foreign and International Law

Before World War II, few U.S. attorneys were involved in foreign and international legal matters. Post-war development of communication, the growth of multinational corporations, and expanded finance, monetary, transportation and trade systems have increased the role that the law of other countries and international law play in American law.

English and Commonwealth Law

The United States legal system has its roots in English common law. In many subjects — such as property — some of the basic principles of law have not changed from early English case law.

This historical interdependence makes English law a source of authority and a reference you will sometimes encounter in your research. Case law from other commonwealth countries like Canada and Australia can also prove useful.

Perhaps the most common reason that you, as an American attorney, will research English law is because you discover the cite of an appropriate English case or statute in an American case, law review or treatise. Many academic libraries have complete sets of English, Canadian and Australian cases and statutes. The citation, plus the guidance of a law librarian, should be enough to lead you to the item. You can also gain access to English materials on the LEXIS service.

English Case Law

If you are approaching English law without known citations, you can use *The Digest, Annotated British, Commonwealth and European Cases* for case annotations and citations. Another approach is via *Halsbury's Law of England*, an encyclopedia of English law which provides citations to cases and statutes. These traditional indexes will cite you to the *Law Reports*, the selective semi-official reporter, and the *All England Law Reports*, a privately printed, comprehensive reporter.

You can also search for published and unpublished cases using the full-text, English General library of the LEXIS service.[11]

English Statutory Law

Although the official statutory compilation for England is *Statutes in Force*, most researchers use *Halsbury's Statutes of England* to access English statutory law because it is much easier to use. *Halsbury's* is comparable to American codifications in the arrangement of laws by subject. The laws are also found in the LEXIS service in the English General library.

Do not confuse statutes with statutory instruments, the English term for regulations and subordinate legislation. Statutory Instruments are found in the official publication *Statutory Instruments*, the private publication *Halsbury's Statutory Instruments*, and in the English General library of the LEXIS service.

■ Basic databases in English and Commonwealth law:

United Kingdom Law libraries on the LEXIS service:
English General library
New Zealand library
Australian library
Commonwealth Case library

Canada has two major commercial legal databases: QL and CAN/LAW. QL includes headnotes from the provincial courts and full-text decisions of some provincial courts, the Federal Court of Canada, and the Supreme Court of Canada. In 1987 Canada Law Book Inc. created CAN/LAW, a database of court decisions reported by the publisher.

SOQUIJ, Societe Quebecoise d'Information Juridique, is maintained by the Quebec Ministry of Justice to cover its provincial materials.[12]

---

[11]The English library is listed on the second page of the LEXIS library menu.

[12]For more information on these databases *see* THE CANADIAN LAW INFORMATION COUNCIL, THE CLIC GUIDE TO COMPUTER-ASSISTED LEGAL RESEARCH (2d rev. ed.).

■ Additional readings in English and Commonwealth legal research:

Margaret A. Banks, *Using a Law Library: A Guide for Students and Lawyers in the Common Law Provinces of Canada* (4th ed. 1985).

Douglass T. MacEllven, *Legal Research Handbook* (2d ed., 1986).

"English and Canadian Materials," Chapter 19 in *How to Find the Law* (8th ed., 1983).

"English Legal Research," Chapter 21 in *Fundamentals of Legal Research* (1987 ed.).

The Law of Other Countries

Unless your practice becomes highly specialized you will not advise your clients on foreign law. However, you may have the need to be familiar with a particular country and its laws, if only to discuss a matter with foreign counsel.

It can be extremely difficult to research foreign law. You will have to first understand the country's legal system so you can identify the sources of law and their relative authority.

Language can create a problem. Translations are helpful but not authoritative. Even if you limit your foreign law research to English speaking countries, you must be aware that legal terminology can vary from the definitions you are accustomed to as an American lawyer. Some of the leading multilingual dictionaries are the *Multilingual Law Dictionary*[13] and the *Legal Dictionary in Four Languages.*[14]

■ Basic research and sources in the law of other countries:

Identifying a country's legal system is basic to researching its law. If a country has a civil law system it will depend more on codifications and less on judicial precedent.

Among the basic sources of law from other jurisdictions is the *Martindale-Hubbell Law Directory*. Volume VIII provides a concise digest of the law of various foreign jurisdictions. The major intent of *Martindale-Hubbell* is to provide the type of general information an American attorney would need to consider when dealing with a problem based in the law of another country.

Two good background sources are Volume I of the *International Encyclopedia of Comparative Law*[15] which includes descrip-

9

---

[13]EGBERT and MORALES-MACEDO, MULTILINGUAL LAW DICTIONARY (1978).

[14]LEDOCTE, LEGAL DICTIONARY IN FOUR LANGUAGES (2d ed., 1978).

[15]*INTERNATIONAL ENCYCLOPEDIA OF COMPARATIVE LAW* is published under the auspices of the International Association of Legal Science. Although its publication has been erratic and is currently on hold, it remains a basic source.

tions of foreign legal systems, and *Major Legal Systems in the World Today*. [16] These two titles help you understand the country's legal system and the type of authority you should expect to find in your research.

Scholarly commentary has special influence in civil law countries. The *Index to Foreign Legal Periodicals* provides access to many of the leading foreign journals.

- Basic databases in the law of other countries:

The French Law libraries in the LEXIS service provide the most comprehensive single source of French case law and regulations available online. Note that the materials in these libraries and the search connectors are in French.

A few European countries have experimented with the development of legal databases but none are readily available to attorneys practicing in the United States.

International Law

Public international law involves the relationships which exist among countries. The primary sources of international law include treaties, other international agreements, decisions of international courts, adjudications and arbitrations. Custom and generally recognized principles of law also play an important role in international law.

As previously mentioned, language and special terminology can be a problem in approaching international law. A good new source is *The International Law Dictionary*. [17]

If your international research involves an organization, like the European Economic Community, you should familiarize yourself with the authorities and documentation the organization produces.

- Basic sources in international law:

M. Akehurst, *A Modern Introduction to International Law* (6th rev. ed., 1987).

I. Brownlie, *Principles of Public International Law* (3d. ed, 1979).

Max Planck Institute for Comparative Public Law and for International Law, *Encyclopedia of Public International Law* (1981 -).

Dept. of the Army, *Law of Peace* (Pam. #27-161-1, 1979).

---

[16] R. DAVID & J. E. BRIERLY, MAJOR LEGAL SYSTEMS IN THE WORLD TODAY (3rd ed. 1985).

[17] R. BLEDSOE & B. BOEZEK, THE INTERNATIONAL LAW DICTIONARY (1987). The dictionary provides thorough definitions of terms.

I. Kavass, *International Business Transactions: A Guide to Research Sources* (1973).

A. Sprudzs, *Treaty Sources in Legal and Political Research* (1973).

- Basic databases in international law:

The following libraries are available on the LEXIS service, and are pertinent to research in international law:

European Communities library: Cases determined in the Court of Justice of the European Community.

International Trade library: Includes decisions and findings of the International Trade Commission, BNA *International Trade Reporter*, and decisions of the Court of International Trade.

- Basic research in international law:

Until 1950 U.S. treaties were included in the *Statutes at Large*. They have been reprinted in *Treaties and Other International Agreements of the United States, 1776 -1949.*[18] You can find more recent treaties in *United States Treaties and other International Agreements.*

Other sources of treaty information:

Department of State Bulletin: The official record of U.S. foreign policy, it provides information on developments in U.S. foreign relations and the work of the Department of State and the Foreign Service. The *Bulletin* is available in full text in the LEXIS service.

International Legal Materials: Published by the American Society of International Law, this is often the first place a treaty appears. It is a must for any lawyer involved in international law.

- Additional information on international legal research can be found in:

Chapter 20, "International Law," in *Fundamentals of Legal Research* (1987 ed.).

Chapter 20, "Foreign and Comparative Law," Chapter 21, "International Law", *How to Find the Law*, 8th ed.

"AALL Institute on International Law and Business," *76 L. Lib. J. 421* (1983).

J. W. Williams, "Guide to International Legal Research," *20 Geo. Wash. J. Int. L. & Econ. 1* (1986).

A. Sprudzs, "International Legal Research: An Infinite Paper Chase," *16 Vand. J. Transnat'l L. 521* (1983).

---

[18] C. BEVANS, TREATIES AND OTHER INTERNATIONAL AGREEMENTS OF THE UNITED STATES, 1776-1949 (1968-1976).

Summary

An attorney always has a responsibility to research a question thoroughly, identifying the ruling authorities and examining the legal issues and possibilities. Specialized research creates unique challenges that can be met through the use of specialized research tools.

This chapter mentions only a few areas of specialization and some of the resources available both in traditional resources and online. It is not comprehensive, but illustrates the wide variety of specialized sources available to legal researchers.

As your own research leads you into new areas of specialization, you will identify "favorite" resources that are dependable, informative, and essential to your practice.

Before you begin to do specialized research or clerk for an office, firm, or government agency that specializes in a particular field of law, become familiar with the appropriate looseleaf services and LEXIS libraries. They can be invaluable.

The Synthesis of Legal Research

The purpose of this book, and of law school courses in legal research, is to give you an introduction to the tools attorneys use in performing legal research. If you complement this introduction with the analytical skills and substantive knowledge you are developing in your coursework, you will direct your research intelligently and professionally.

Legal research is a very personalized skill. You might be more comfortable with some research tools or believe one source is more reliable and suitable for your work. You may cling to the traditional tools of legal research or already have your LEXIS ID number memorized.

Regardless of your preferences, when you face a legal problem you should be able to analyze it, gather the appropriate information and synthesize what you have learned to guide your legal action. The result of your research is advice or a recommended legal action for your client. This chapter pulls together the separate discussions of research tools and provides general guidelines on legal research.

Identifying What You Know

Identifying your level of knowledge of the law and what research you must perform on a given issue is a personal decision — only you know what you do not know. Deciding how much research to perform can be a very humbling experience, particularly if you are billing a client to find what seems to be the answer to a basic question.

Keep the audience in mind. Although all legal research should be thorough, you prepare differently for a local traffic court hearing than for an argument before the U.S. Supreme Court.

"I Know Nothing"

If you totally lack experience in the area of law, ask two questions:

1) Should I refer the client to an attorney who practices in the area of law? (Some areas, such as corporate pension law, have become very complex in recent years, and require a working knowledge of the administration of several major acts of Congress.)

2) Is the problem one I can solve by educating myself?

If you are working for a court, law firm or agency, the research decision may not be for you to make. If a judge, partner or supervising attorney asks you to research an issue in an area of law that is unfamiliar, you must know how to learn the law. However, if you are a single practitioner and a client has a complex pension issue, the decision on whether to research or refer is very much yours. Your only other guide is your professional obligation described in Chapter One.[1]

If you are confident you can learn the law, first become familiar with the legal concepts and language used in that area of law. Identify a leading treatise, hornbook or law review article that provides background. Many people gain an overview of a legal topic by reading the outline and synopses provided by a legal encyclopedia or annotated digest. Identifying a relevant A.L.R. annotation can be a tremendous aid, providing an overall description of the law, analysis, practice advice and cites to pertinent authorities.

You can use the LEXIS service or traditional indexes to find an overview of the law in law reviews or A.L.R. annotations. You also can use law review indexes in online or printed form. The choice is yours.

The LEXIS service can help you begin your research.

The full-text searching capabilities of the LEXIS service in case law can be helpful as a starting tool. Give yourself five minutes with the goal of finding a recent case that analyzes the issues and summarizes the law. Such a case may not exist. So, if you are not successful, do not continue to search aimlessly. It is worth your time if you find a good case early in your research. If you do not, switch to another LEXIS file or another tool.

"I Can State the Issues"

If you are comfortable with the issues, concepts and language involved in the problem, you can use the checklist described in Chapter Three to identify the appropriate sources of law.

Given the issues, what is the jurisdiction? Would you expect common law or a statute to determine the law? Is this an area in

---

[1]See pages 1-2.

which you expect to find administrative regulations? For example, in the Tax Problem and the Explosive Problem you can expect to find a criminal statute.

Sometimes in the beginning of your research you are uncertain of the sources you should use. In the Billboard Problem, the uncertainty of jurisdiction actually defines the issue — should you look to federal law or state law to determine if the billboards can be built on an Indian reservation? Research in the Billboard Problem delineates the issue of which law applies and assists you in looking to constitutional principles to resolve the issue.

Identify the possible sources of law and how you expect to find them before you begin research. Such a strategy avoids a premature conclusion that you have found the answer after consulting just one source of law. It is usual for a description of the law pertaining to a problem to include a blend of case, statutory, administrative and constitutional law.

Avoid a premature conclusion that you have found the answer in just one source of law.

Practical Advice on Legal Research

Advice on Case Research

The practice you gain throughout law school in applying principles of common law will serve you well in case research.

The first step is identifying the jurisdiction. Could courts with international, federal, state or local jurisdiction decide the issues? Often more than one jurisdiction may interpret the law for your problem.[2] Be certain you search all possible LEXIS files and indexes for all possible reporter series.

After you list possible jurisdictions, envision a relevant case. Think of how an editor might have categorized the case under digest headings. Think of the pattern of words in the case that could be described by a LEXIS search.

Reading cases is one of the best means of understanding the law. Court opinions often summarize the law, analyzing and applying statutes and precedent. You also can rely on the research of the parties and court, as their briefs and opinions will cite other pertinent authorities.

Advice on Statutory Research

At the beginning of research, you should assume a statute applies to your problem. Statutes can modify virtually every area of common law. So, assume a statute applies to your problem until you

---

[2]The court of another state or a federal court often may interpret the law of a state. A search for a state law issue in federal case files or case files of another state may find additional authority. To find instances of courts applying the law of another jurisdiction, e.g., federal or state courts applying Illinois law,

TRANSMIT: *illinois* W/3 *case* OR *law* OR *statute*

are satisfied none does apply.

The first question you should ask is whether international, federal, state or local government law applies. The elements of the checklist should guide you to the possible sources. If any of the elements involve another country, you must consider the possible jurisdiction and application of the law of that country.

It is advisable to use both an index and full-text searching in your statutory research. Stilted statutory language can sometimes obscure a relevant section from the indexer or the full-text searcher.

To help understand what the law was intended to accomplish, consider the legislative history of the statute.

To understand how a statute has been applied, consider how courts and administrative agencies have interpreted the statute in specific fact situations. A variety of complementary sources are available. Annotated codes cite to cases and other sources. A LEXIS search through case and administrative law may find additional and more recent materials. Shepardize the statute. Finally, search secondary and non-legal sources for references to the statute that may describe the most recent enforcement actions or policies.

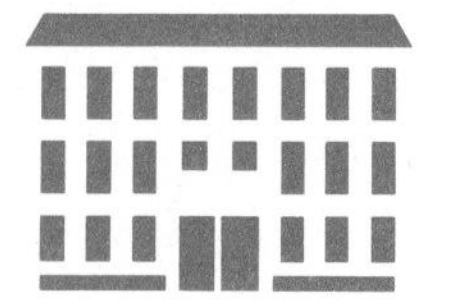

Advice on Research in Administrative Law

Today an attorney must recognize the potential impact of administrative law on every issue. You must be aware of the role state and federal administrative agencies play in defining, interpreting and enforcing the law. Finding administrative law involves finding regulations, administrative decisions and case law interpreting the regulations, and predicting the actions of the offices responsible for enforcing the regulations.

Some attorneys practice almost exclusively within the purview of a federal agency and rely mainly on regulations and other administrative sources of law. But sometimes lawyers fail to consider the possibility that administrative regulations might affect their client's situation. For example, a real estate lawyer might forget to determine how regulations issued by the Federal Aviation Administration may affect the use of a client's property near an airport.

Administrative questions are often addressed by a looseleaf service or specialized LEXIS library covering a particular area of law. Once you have identified the pertinent LEXIS library or looseleaf service, a big part of your research is done!

Advice on Research in Developing Areas of Law

Your client or manager may present you with a legal question that has no authoritative answer. The question may involve an area of law that is developing, perhaps amid controversy, and no court or legislative body has provided a definitive opinion or statute that can be followed.

Such a situation can be exciting, particularly if it provides you an opportunity to argue the issues and help create law. You may attempt to apply existing authorities in ways they have not been applied before. You may be in search of an aspect or fact in legal precedents that may not have been given serious consideration before you saw the application to your problem. For example, the early law pertaining to automobiles looked to aspects of the law of carriages for precedents that could apply. The law of electronic publishing looks to aspects of traditional publishing for principles and analogous situations. Your ability to formulate searches for facts or aspects of prior authorities is limited only by your ability to develop reasoned approaches and arguments.

You can look to law reviews and legal journals, which often identify, discuss and even influence developing areas of law.

Consider the NEXIS service when faced with a problem for which the law is developing or for which recent developments may not be reported in traditional legal sources. The newspapers, magazines, newsletters, wire services and other sources included in the NEXIS service may report on out-of-court settlements, social issues, research and technical developments, litigations in process and otherwise unreported trials.

Updating Your Research

Now is the time to develop the discipline to always attempt to find more recent authority. Check the pocket parts and advance sheets of all sources. Use Shepard's, either in hard copy or online, to trace the citation history of the authority you have found. Use Auto-Cite to be certain the citation is accurate and that the case is still good law.

If you started your research several days ago, go back to the online services, pocket parts and advance sheets to make certain the law has not changed. Retracing your steps when you update your research means that you need a good, written record of what those steps were.

If you started your research several days ago, update the research by retracing your steps.

Coordinating Hard Copy and Computer-Assisted Legal Research

It would be too obvious for a publication sponsored by LEXIS to tout the benefits of computer-assisted legal research. You need to understand the capabilities of both hard copy and online services to intelligently use both for your clients' benefit. Each research tool described in this book has advantages over others for certain research functions.[3] Those advantages cannot all be neatly catego-

[3]For one synopsis see S.A. Childress, *The Hazards of Computer-Assisted Research to the Legal Profession*, 55 OKLA. B.J. 1531 (1984).

rized. In some instances the LEXIS service has found crucial authority that was not found in hours of research with other tools. In other instances the LEXIS service has assisted in verifying results, but neither saved time nor found additional authority.

Sometimes you have no choice — your firm does not have access to computer-assisted research — and you are limited to the hardcopy tools in your firm or local law library. However, more and more firms, agencies and businesses are using online services. These organizations often are relying on the expertise of recent law graduates to utilize the new services.[4] You should be ready to use both the hard copy and computer-assisted services.

Using the LEXIS service at the beginning of your research can save you time by enabling you to search your precise issue, find relevant authorities in several different sources of law, find recent authorities first and verify that the authority you find is good law — all in the initial session. But do not start by signing on. Begin by going through the process described in Chapter Three, identifying the critical elements of your problem and devising a LEXIS search strategy before you go online. Do not waste your clients' money by choosing the files and formulating the search while using the terminal.

The LEXIS service can save you time in finding pertinent authorities in several sources of law. Choose the LEXIS files you will search for primary and secondary authorities by using the *LEXIS/NEXIS Library Contents and Alphabetical List of Files.*[5] Consider the specialized libraries that group together authorities on a subject. For example, your chances of finding pertinent authorities to resolve the Tax Problem are enhanced if you begin in the LEXIS Federal Tax library. Knowing that you are searching through tax materials enables you to search for occurrences of the words that will be unique to your problem, without adding terms only to eliminate cases outside the area of tax.

---

[4]Many law students and recent graduates note their proficiency in computer-assisted research on their resumes.

[5]A list of files is also available online. All LEXIS subscribers can use the online version at a reduced rate.

At any point in a LEXIS session, you can direct your research into many different sources and tools in just one or two steps. For example, the following is a LEXIS screen of a Supreme Court case. Following the screen is a partial list of possible next steps.

```
        480 U.S. 557; 107 S. Ct. 1410; 1987 U.S. LEXIS 1385; 94 L. Ed. 2d. 563;

the several States . . . shall be liable in damages to any person suffering
injury while he is employed by such carrier in such commerce . . . resulting in
whole or in part from the negligence of any of the officers, agents, or
employees of such carrier, or by reason of any defect or insufficiency, due to
its negligence, in its cars, engines, appliances, machinery, tract, roadbed,
works, boats, wharves, or other equipment." 45 U.S.C. § 51.

   n8 Thus, for example, with respect to causation, we have held that "the test
of a jury case" under the statute is "simply whether the proofs justify with
reason the conclusion that employer negligence played any part, even the
slightest, in producing the injury or death for which damages are sought."
Rogers v. Missouri Pacific R. Co., 352 U.S. 500, 506 (1957).  Indeed, in the
spirit of broad construction, the FELA has been construed to cover some
intentional torts even though its text only mentions negligence.  See Jamison v.
Encarnacion, 281 U.S. 635, 641 (1930); Lancaster v. Norfolk and Western R. Co.,
773 F.2d 807, 812-813 (CA7 1985), cert. pending No. 85-1702; Slaughter v.
Atlantic Coast Line R. Co., 112 U.S. App. D.C. 327, 302 F.2d 912, cert denied,
371 U.S. 827 (1962); see generally Annotation, Liability Under Federal
Employers' Liability Act for Intentional Tort, 8 ALR 3d 442 (1966).  [*9]

   The RLA, by contrast, provides a comprehensive framework for the resolution
of labor disputes in the railroad industry.  Enacted in 1926, the text of the
```

- View the Auto-Cite entry for 480 U.S. 557:
  TRANSMIT: *ac*
- View the Shepard's entry for 480 U.S. 557:
  TRANSMIT: *shep*
- View the next page of the opinion:
  PRESS the NEXT PAGE key
- View the next retrieved case (if any):
  PRESS the NEXT CASE key
- View the full text of 45 U.S.C. § 51 in U.S.C.S.:
  TRANSMIT: *lexstat 45 usc 51*
- View the text of the *Rogers* case, 352 U.S. 500:
  TRANSMIT: *lexsee 352 U.S. 500*
- View the text of the annotation, 8 A.L.R.3d 442:
  TRANSMIT: *lexsee 8 alr3d 442*
- View the Auto-Cite entry for the A.L.R. annotation:
  TRANSMIT: *ac 8 alr3d 442*
- Change to the LEXIS library of law reviews:
  PRESS the CHG LIB key and TRANSMIT: *lawrev*

Some of the options available to a legal researcher viewing the LEXIS screen shown above.

Compare the coverage of the research tools you choose. A legal database may be necessary if the documents you need to search are otherwise unavailable to you. If your library does not have the necessary reporter series or state code, or if the reporter series does not report some cases, you should determine if the LEXIS service has the sources.

If coverage is equivalent, compare the capabilities of the available tools to your research needs. How would you determine if the California courts have ever used the phrase "commercial speech" in an opinion? How would you determine if Justice Blackmun has ever used the phrase "commercial speech" in one of his opinions?

Compare the results to determine if another tool finds additional authority.

The best way for determining the relative merits of different research tools is to compare the results you find with each tool. Then determine whether the cause of your failure to find certain authorities with a tool was due to the tool or the way you used it. Another very good reason for comparing the results of your research with the various hard copy and computer-assisted services is to verify that your research has been thorough.

Develop a checklist of the tools you use. You can refer to the tools as you begin a new research problem. For instance, you may wonder if a clause similar to the one you are drafting has ever been the object of a litigation. Refer to your checklist to determine the best tools to use.

Research Tools Checklist

index to code
LEXIS to search code
digest
LEXIS to search cases
ALR Quick Index
LEXIS to search A.L.R. annotations
Index to legal Periodicals
Legal Resource Index
hornbooks/treatises (check card catalog)
Shepard's
Auto-Cite
LEXIS as a citator
C.F.R. Index
L. Ed. Supreme Court Digest

When to Stop

Just as it is difficult to discern when you have considered all the substantive and procedural theories, it is difficult to determine when you have exhausted all avenues of legal research. Research should always be pursued zealously, yet there is a point beyond which more research will be of marginal benefit to your client. Often at that point each authority you find cites to the authorities you have already found.

Common Mistakes

What are the common mistakes people tend to make performing legal research? The most basic mistake is failing to perform any research. The following are some common errors of students and attorneys:

- Finding an answer and ending the research, ignoring other sources which could provide more information or even a different answer
- Floundering aimlessly, reading bits and pieces of law before gaining an understanding of the area of law
- Forgetting to check the pocket parts or supplements
- Failing to update a citation
- Concluding "there is no case" after checking one digest topic or running one search
- Relying on a description of a case holding without reading the case
- Failing to keep a short-hand record of sources and topics checked
- Failing to include alternative forms of expression in a search request, forgetting synonyms or truncated forms of a word
- Failing to identify all the LEXIS files which could contain pertinent information
- Rejecting a retrieved case before a thorough reading
- Failing to print the request, results and date to use in later follow-up
- Failing to verify citations using LEXIS, Auto-Cite and Shepard's

Time and Cost as Considerations in Legal Research

Time is an issue in many aspects of legal research. The amount of time you have may determine when you stop, e.g., when you must meet a filing deadline. Your time is also a financial consideration for your client. How much time can you afford to give a problem and how much of your time can a client afford?[6] In most circumstances it is not sensible to bill a client $700 to resolve a potential liability of $500.

[6]There has been a concern that database searching is available only to large firms and government agencies which can afford to subscribe to the services. Competitive pricing, new competing services and new means of subscribing through sponsoring organizations have made computer-asssisted tools affordable to smaller firms.

As you become familiar with the benefits of finding legal information when you need it, you will have a better realization of the economic impact of research costs on your practice. A search in a specialized LEXIS library or the purchase of a looseleaf service may seem expensive until you understand the valuable time savings or the importance of the results found.

Avoid quick cost calculations that categorize a problem as a "book" problem or an "online" problem. Attorneys who do so create limitations on their research because they are not properly integrating computer-assisted research with their use of traditional research tools.

Some of the cost of legal research is not immediately apparent. For example, if you purchase legal books you should also buy the supplementation that keeps the set up to date. The rising cost of office space for shelving is another cost factor which is often overlooked.

It is difficult to compare these ongoing expenses of legal research with the more readily apparent cost of paying for each use, as you incur when you search an online service for a specific issue and charge the client for the search. A law firm may prefer to pay for the cost of each use, as it makes business and ethical sense to bill research costs directly to the client that gains from the research.

Summary

This Manual has been written to assist you in developing your skills as a legal researcher and in integrating computer-assisted research with traditional research tools. May it be helpful, not only in your first year of law school, but throughout your legal career.

Index

A

B

C

T

U

V

W